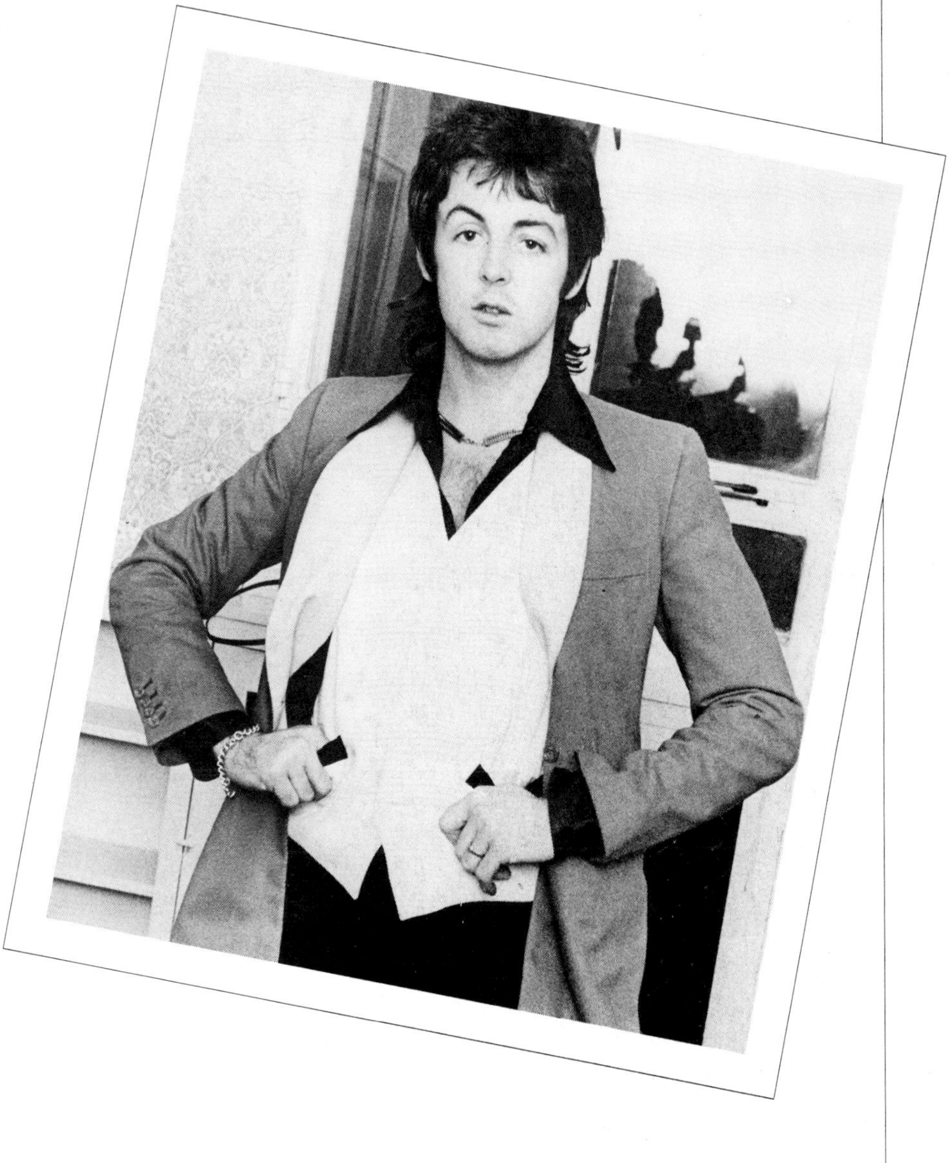

OMNIBUS PRESS
London / New York / Paris / Sydney

The bulk of this book was recorded in conversations with Paul McCartney held during the last two months of 1973. The *Venus & Mars* section stands alone, written summer 1975.

This book is dedicated to Scott, Andrew and Walters, with love to Janice.

(A Division of Book Sales Limited).
ISBN 0-7119-5494-1 Order No.OP47813
Written & edited by Paul Gambaccini.
Text pages designed by Pearce Marchbank.

Exclusive Distributors
Book Sales Limited, 8/9 Frith Street, London W1V 5TZ, UK.
Music Sales Corporation, 257 Park Avenue South, New York, NY 10010, USA.
Music Sales Pty Limited, 120 Rothschild Avenue, Rosebery, NSW 2018, Australia.
To the Music Trade only:
Music Sales Limited, 8/9 Frith Street, London W1V 5TZ, UK.

Photo credits: Cover by Steven Pyke, courtesy of MPL Communications, Camera Press: 19, 22, 24, 29, 33, 35, 36, 38, 41, 42(inset), 53, 53(inset), 67(inset), 101; Henry Diltz: 86, 98-99; Robert Ellis: 88-89; Robin Katz: 81; London Express: 72; London Features International: 61, 82, 91, 95 97(inset), 80(inset), 82(inset), 83, 91(inset), 92(inset), 96, 104(inset), 111; Linda McCartney: 49, 52, 63(inset), 66; Miles Archives: 18, 28; Rex Features: 11, 12-13, 14, 16(inset), 20, 21(inset), 25, 26-27, 30-31, 42, 62, 68, 102; Kate Simon: 6-7, 76-77, 108(inset), 109; SKR Photos: 5(insets); Joe Stevens: 4-5, 54(inset), 63, 70, 70(inset), 75, 75(inset), 80(inset), 82(inset), 83, 91(inset), 92(inset), 96, 104(inset), 111; Adrian Boot: 112

Every effort has been made to trace the copyright holders of the photographs in this book but one or two were unreachable. We would be grateful if the photographers concerned would contact us.

Printed in the United Kingdom by Scotprint, Musselburgh, Edinburgh.

A catalogue record for this book is available from the British Library.

6
11

PAUL AND LINDA WITH DAVID FROST.

McCARTNEY THE LAD: BUTLINS TO HAMBURG.

The first time I ever sang on a stage I did 'Long Tall Sally.' I must have been pretty young, probably 14. I might have been 11, I don't know. We went to stay with our parents at a holiday camp named Butlins, a branch in Wales. They used to have these talent shows, and one of my cousins-in-law was one of the red coats who had something to do with the entertainment. He called us up on the stage. I had my guitar with me. Looking back on it, it must have been a put-up job, I don't know what I was doing there with my guitar. I probably asked him to get me up. I went up with my brother Mike, who had just recovered from breaking his arm and looked all pale. He had his arm in a big sling. We used to do an Everly Brothers number, something like 'Bye Bye Love.' I think it might have been 'Bye Bye Love,' in fact. We did that, and then I finished with 'Long Tall Sally.'

Ever since I heard Little Richard's version, I started imitating him. It was just straight imitation, really, which has gradually become my version of it as much as Richard's. I started doing it in one of the classrooms at school, it was just one of the imitations I could do well. I could do Fats Domino, I could do Elvis, I could do a few people. (Smiles.) I still can! "I'm walking, yes indeed, I'm . . ." (Fats Domino impersonation) "Thank you very much, ladies and gentlemen," (Elvis Presley impersonation) That's Elvis.

'Long Tall Sally' is all this stuff I used to do. I could never think of a better number to finish on. There was a time when we didn't do it, we used to do 'What'd I Say.' Then that ran out and I used to do a crazy version of 'Hey Bob a Rebop.' It was anything, really, to get the audience going. (Sings 'Hey Bop a Rebop.') The "hey's were like in 'What'd I Say.' "Ye...ahhh! Ye...ahhh!" But none of them excelled 'Long Tall Sally,' which is why I still do it.

When you wrote 'I'm Down' you did it in Little Richard's style.

That was to replace 'Long Tall Sally' as a finisher, a big loud rocky number. That was, as a painter would say, after Little Richard.

Did many of those black artists appeal to you in the late fifties and early sixties? John did several Motown songs.

Yes, very much. I loved all that stuff. Those were my favourites, definitely.

Did the Cunard Yanks (Britons on Atlantic ship crossings) have anything to do with introducing you to these records?

I don't think so. They might have, but originally you just heard a few songs that came up. They were so different from what had gone before. In England, one of the guys who started it was a guy called Lonnie Donegan. He was doing it, and then simultaneously there was this music coming in from America, Chuck Berry, Fats Domino, Little Richard, Elvis, Gene Vincent, Eddie Cochran.

Then we used to get a few films coming in, like 'Rock Around the Clock', 'Don't Knock the Rock', 'Twist Around the Clock', 'Girl Can't Help It', a few of them, and those were kind of, wow. In fact, I remember George and I going to see *Blackboard Jungle.* George was fifteen at the time and you had to be sixteen to go and see it. But I was sixteen, so I was all right. George's mum was saying "You'll never get in, you'll never get in," and we were saying "Don't worry, we'll get him in." We went out into the back garden and got a bit of mud. George had the buddings of a little moustache so he rubbed mud on his moustache. We went along to the picture house and we got in. "Sure, he's sixteen" . . . we spoke a bit deeper. The only reason we were

PAUL AND HIS BROTHER MICHAEL.

going was because a Bill Haley song, 'Rock Around the Clock,' was in the film. That's the only reason we went to see the film, that one song.

You've mentioned being emotionally affected by music at the age of five. What were your influences at that time?

I used to listen to the radio a lot, so I used to like popular music. And I got all the old music from films, Fred Astaire and stuff like that, which I loved.

George Martin said that you sang 'Over the Rainbow' at one point.

Yes, I used to do all those kind of songs. I used to do 'Till There Was You,' I used to do 'Over the Rainbow.' I only did that because Gene Vincent did it and it was Gene Vincent's version that turned me on, not Judy's, although I knew hers from the film (*Wizard of Oz* starring Judy Garland).

From a very early age I was interested in singing tunes. I like a nice tune. You know, 'White Christmas,' 'Over the Rainbow,' the old stuff. My Dad used to play a lot, so I suppose I was quite influenced by him. 'Stairway to Paradise' and 'Chicago,' tunes like that, the old jazz tunes. He used to have a band, my Dad. He used to have a band called Jim Mac's Band. That was when he was about 25. He had to give it up eventually because he got false teeth and couldn't play the trumpet.

When did you first think you wanted to be in a band?

I don't think I wanted to be in one. I wanted to do something in music and my Dad gave me a trumpet for my birthday. I went through trying to learn that. But my mouth used to get too sore. You know, you have to go through a period of getting your lip hard. I suddenly realized that I wouldn't be able to sing if I played trumpet. So I figured guitar would be better. It was about the time that guitar was beginning to be *the* instrument. So I went and swapped my trumpet for a guitar and I got that home and couldn't figure out what was wrong and I suddenly decided to turn the strings around and that made a difference and I realized I was left-handed. I started from there, really; that was my first kind of thing, and then once you had a guitar you were then kind of eligible for bands. But I never thought of myself being in a band.

One day I went with this friend of mine. His name was Ivan (Vaughan). I went up to Woolton, in Liverpool, and there was a village fete on, and John and his friends were playing for the thing. My friend Ivan knew John, who was a neighbour of his. And we met there and John was onstage singing "Come little darlin', come and go with me . . ." *'The Del Vikings' 'Come Go With Me'?*

But he never knew the words because he didn't know the record, so he made up his own words, like "down, down, down, down to the penitentiary." I remember I was impressed. I thought, wow, he's good. That's a good band there. So backstage, back in the church hall later,

IN LIVERPOOL 1963 AND (INSET) ON STAGE IN HAMBURG.

PAUL WITH HIS FATHER JIM McCARTNEY.

THE BEATLES PLAYING THE CAVERN

GEORGE, JOHN AND PAUL IN LIVERPOOL.

I was singing a couple of songs I'd known.

I used to know all the words to 'Twenty Flight Rock' and a few others and it was pretty much in those days to know the words to that. John didn't know the words to many songs, so I was valuable. I wrote up a few words and showed him how to play 'Twenty Flight Rock' and another one, I think. He played all this stuff and I remember thinking he smelled a bit drunk. Quite a nice chap, but he was still a bit drunk. Anyway, that was my first introduction, and I sang a couple of old things.

I liked their band, and then one of their friends who was in the band, a guy named Pete Shotton who was a friend of John's, saw me cycling up in Woolton one day and said "Hey, they said they'd quite like to have you in the band, if you'd like to join." I said "Oh, yeah, it'd be great." We then met up somewhere and I was in the band.

I was originally on guitar. The first thing we had was at a Conservative Club somewhere in Broadway, which is an area of Liverpool, as well as New York. There was a Conservative Club there and I had a big solo, a guitar boogie. I had this big solo and it came to my bit and I blew it. I blew it. Sticky fingers, you know. I couldn't play at all and I got terribly embarrassed. So, I goofed that one terribly, so from then on I was on rhythm guitar. Blown out on lead!

We went to Hamburg, and I had a real cheap guitar, an electric guitar. It finally blew up on me, it finally fell apart in Hamburg. It just wasn't used to being like that. Then I was on piano for a little while. So I went from bass to lead guitar to rhythm guitar to piano. I used to do a few numbers like Ray Charles 'Don't Let the Sun Catch You Crying' and a couple of Jerry Lee Lewis' like 'High School Confidential.'

Then Stuart (Sutcliffe) left the group. He was the bass player. He lent me his bass, and I played bass for a few weeks. I used to play it upside down. And he used to have piano strings on it, because you couldn't get bass strings. They were a bit rare, you know, and they cost a lot, too, about two pounds for one string. So he would cut these big lengths of piano strings from the piano and wind them on the guitar. So I played that upside down for a while. I'm pretty versatile, I'll give that to myself. I wasn't very good, but I was versatile.

I'm in Hamburg, and I have a little bit of money together, and finally saved enough to buy myself a Hofner violin bass. It was my bass, then, that was the one. And I became known for that bass, a lot of kids got them. That was my big pride and joy, because it sounded great.

And that was it, basically. The rest you know.

BEATLES: LIVERPOOL TO THE WORLD.

John and I gradually started to write stuff together. Which didn't mean we wrote everything together. We'd kind of write 80% together and the other 20% for me were things like 'Yesterday' and for John things like 'Strawberry Fields' that he'd write mainly on his own. And I did certain stuff on my own.

When I first started writing songs I started using a guitar. The first one I ever wrote was called 'My Little Girl' which is a funny little song, a nice little song, a corny little song based on three chords – G, G7 and C. A little later we had a piano and I used to bang around on that. I wrote 'When I'm Sixty-Four' when I was about 16. I wrote the tune for that and I was vaguely thinking that it might come in handy in a musical comedy or something. I didn't know what kind of career I was going to take.

So I wrote that on piano and from there it's really been a mixture of both. I just do either, now. Sometimes I've got a guitar in my hands, sometimes I'm sittin' at a piano. It depends whatever instrument I'm at – I'll compose on it, you know.

Do you start with a title or a line, or what?

Oh, different ways. Every time it's different. 'All My Loving' I wrote like a bit of poetry, and then I put a song to it later. Something like 'Yesterday' I did the tune first and wrote words to that later. I called that 'Scrambled Egg' for a long time. I didn't have any words to it. (Sings the melody with the words "scrambled egg . . . da da da da . . . scrambled egg . . .") So then I got words to that; so I say, every time is different, really.

When did you get the idea you were going to bring in a string quartet on 'Scrambled Egg?'

First of all, I was just playing it through for everyone – saying, how do you like this song? I played it just me on acoustic, and sang it. And the rest of the Beatles said, "That's it. Love it." So George Martin and I got together and sort of cooked up this idea. I wanted just a small string arrangement. And he said, "Well, how about your actual string quartet?" I said great, it sounds great. We sat down at a piano and cooked that one up.

Do you feel stronger about that song than the others?

I do, actually, you know. I really reckon 'Yesterday' is probably my best. Don't know why, really, but I think if you do a song that lots of people know, like when you're sitting in a bar and the pianist includes it in his repertoire . . . I was in a shop the other day in Regent Street (London) and they had a pianist in the foyer. I was just looking for some sweaters, and Christmas presents. The pianist was playing all Noel Coward hits. So I went and did all my shopping and he was piped through to all the departments and I thought he was doing a grand job, working his bottom off. On the way out I just leaned over and said "Thank you." I thought he might appreciate it. And he said "You're welcome," and he did appreciate it, actually, and he recognized me and as I'm going out he went (sings melody of 'Yesterday').

I like it not only because it was a big success but because it was one of the most instinctive songs I've ever written. I just rolled out of my bed one morning and there was a piano next to the bed in the place where I was living at the time, and I rolled out of bed and just got the tune. I was so *proud* of it. I felt it was an original tune, it didn't copy off anything, and it was a big tune, it was all there and nothing repeated.

I get made fun of because of it a bit. I remember George saying "Blimey, he's always

EARLY PUBLICITY SHOTS: ON THE MERSEY FERRY AND IN LOOK-ALIKE 'BEATLE JACKETS'.

IN THEIR HOTEL DURING THE FIRST AUSTRALIAN TOUR.

talking about 'Yesterday', you'd think he was Beethoven or somebody." But it is the one, I reckon, that is the most complete thing I've ever written.

It's very catchy without being sickly, too. When you're trying to write a song, there are certain times when you get the essence, it's all there. It's like an egg being laid, it's just so there, not a crack nor a flaw in it.

That song helped make the ballad respectable for rock bands.

I remember old Mick Jagger, saying "Oh, I wish I could sing like that," because at the time he didn't reckon he could. Later, Mick's voice improved a lot.

I like ballads, and I know people like them, too. I'm hip to the fact that people like a love song.

If that's your favourite of your songs, do you have any favourites that you wrote with John?

Lots, actually. I liked 'In My Life.' Those were words that John wrote and I wrote the tune to it. That was a great one. I'm just singling out one there, but there's lots, really. 'Norwegian Wood,' that was mainly John's. But you go through so many . . . I like lots of them. (Thinks a moment.) I like 'Eleanor Rigby,' too, I thought that was a fair one.

Who put the "yeah"s on 'She Loves You'?

John and I wrote it into the song. 'She loves you, yeah, yeah, yeah.' But the idea of having the sixth chord when it finishes was George's. George Harrison's. And George Martin said "That's funny. That's very old fashioned." And we said "Yes, but it's nice, isn't it?" He said "Yes, OK."

PLAYING THE CAVERN.

Then you were praised for your intervals.

Yes, that's right. Aeolic (sic) cadences.

Had you ever heard of them before that?

Nope. Still don't know what it means.

How would you see George Martin's contributions in those songs in those days?

George's contribution was quite a big one, actually. The first time he really ever showed that he could see beyond what we were offering him was 'Please Please Me.' It was originally conceived as a Roy Orbison-type thing, you know. George Martin said "Well, we'll put the tempo up." He lifted the tempo and we all thought that was much better and that was a big hit. George was in there quite heavily from the beginning.

The time we got offended, I'll tell you, was one of the reviews, I think about *Sgt. Pepper* – one of the reviews said, "This is George Martin's finest album." We got shook. I mean, "We don't mind him helping us, it's great, it's a great help, but it's not his album, folks, you know." And there got to be a little bitterness over that. A big help, but Christ, if he's going to get all the credit . . . for the whole album . . . (Paul plays with his children.)

It was one of the first albums that had a continuity. Did you have that in mind when you wrote it?

No. It was just a song called 'Sergeant Pepper's Lonely Hearts Club Band,' made up to open the album. Then we went on to the Billy Shears idea at the end of it and went segue into Ringo's number, and it made the whole thing seem integrated. So we finished the album with it to kind of top-and-tail it, a bit like we've done on

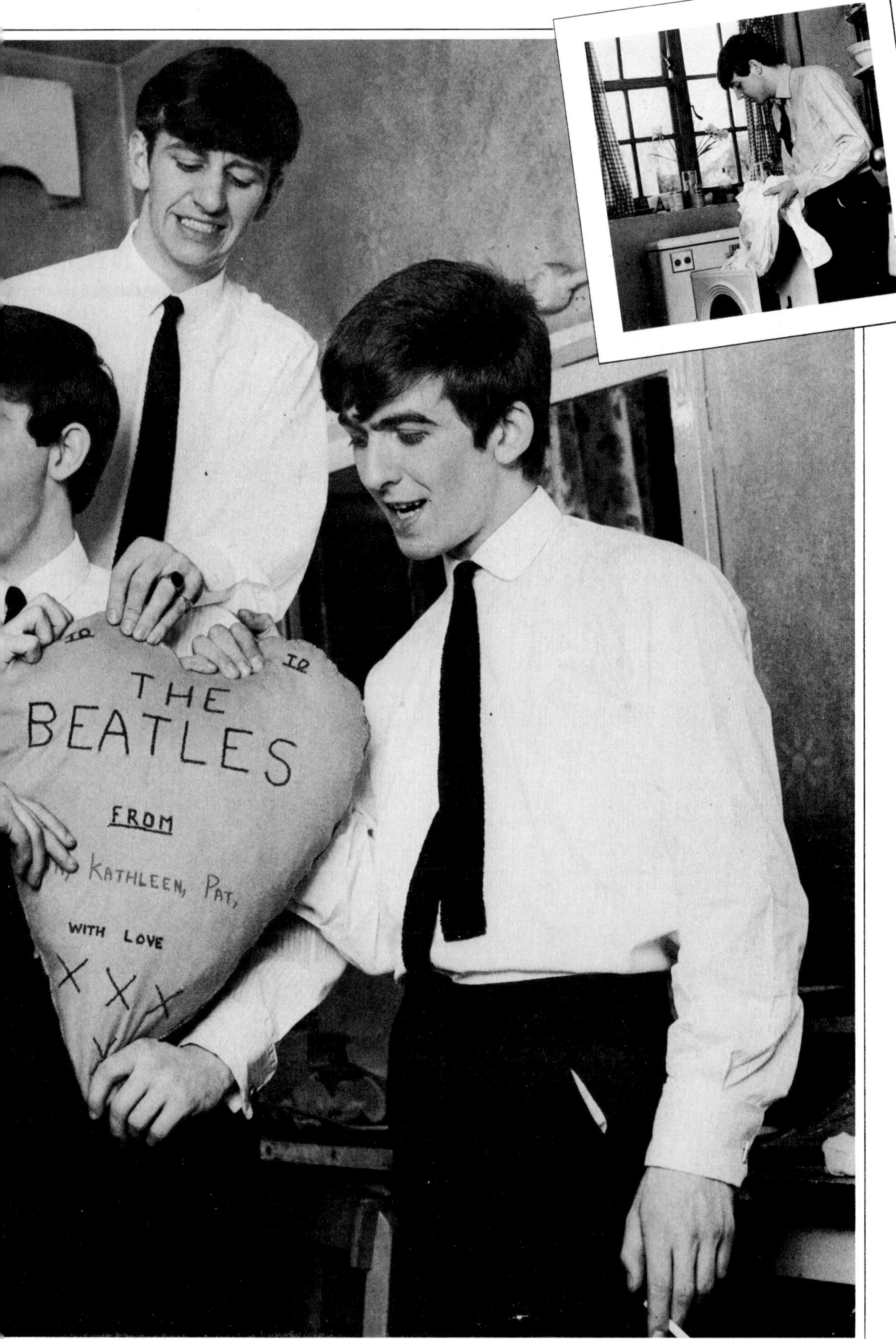
THE
BEATLES
FROM
KATHLEEN, PAT,
WITH LOVE

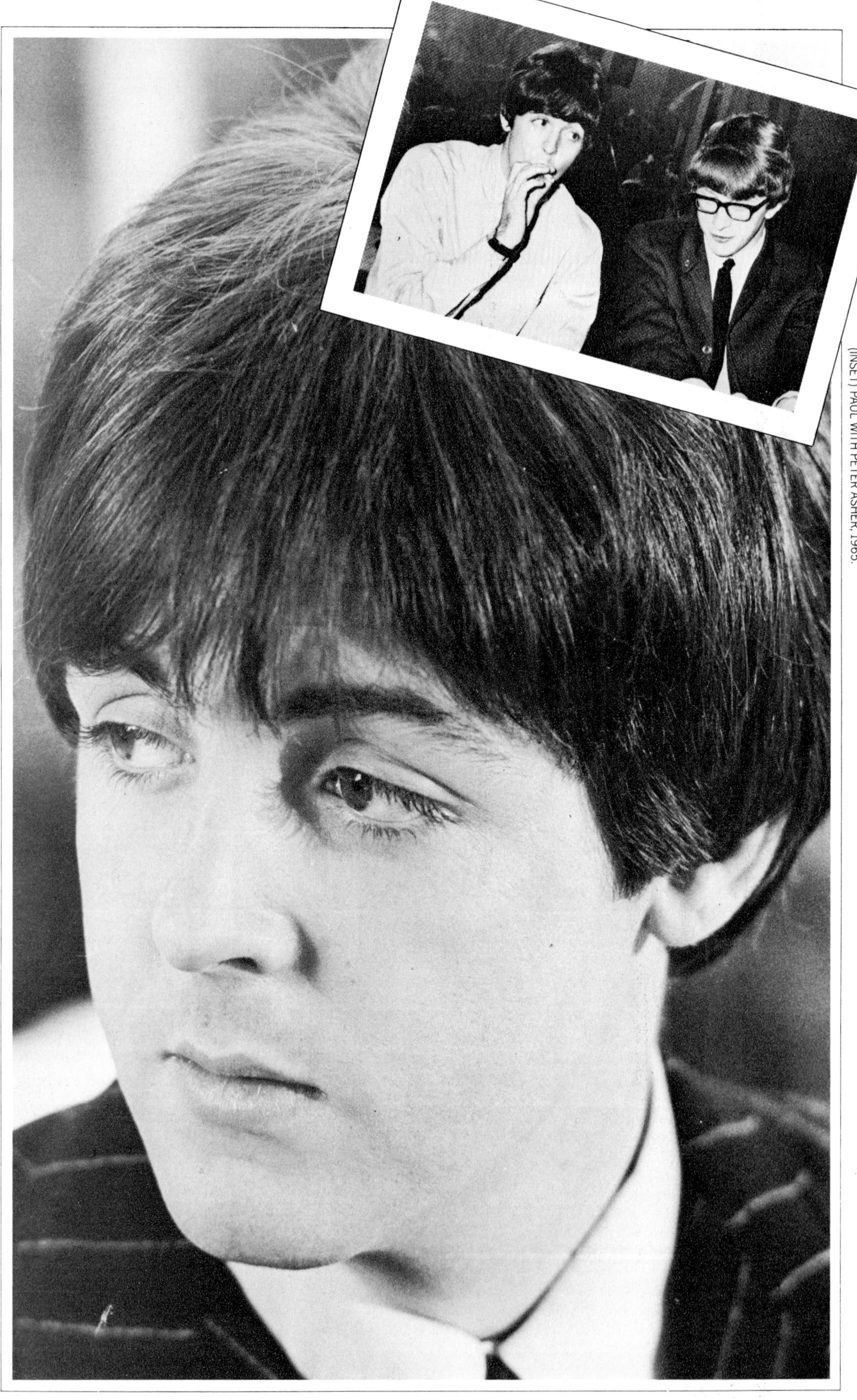

(INSET) PAUL WITH PETER ASHER, 1965.

Band on the Run and, there you go, everyone said "Ah! A concept album!" It was the first time I'd heard the word.

So you didn't see any risk involved in making an album that turned out to be a standard –

It's a goodie.

– And when I say a standard I mean not only on its own merits but a standard against which other albums are compared. Do you laugh when you see that?

No. I'm like most people. You don't laugh, you don't cry, you just see it, you say, oh yeah, '*Sergeant Pepper* of the Seventies.' You just go along with it, you don't think anything.

You wrote the middle bit of 'A Day in the Life' from that album. Had you intended "had a smoke" as a reference to marijuana?

Yeah, it was a kind of risque reference to it. Yes.

Do you think, looking back, that that inspired some people to do something they shouldn't have done?

Probably did, yes. There was a question at the time as to whether we should put it in, publishing be damned, or whether we should be cool and leave it out. It was at the time when everyone was just starting with grass and to just kind of dabble. We thought, "Ah, come on, what the hell, let's put it in." It worked nicely in the song and it was a bit of a thrill for us, just putting something in a song that was like putting something sexy in a song. I didn't realize and I don't really know whether it had that big an effect. It possibly did. We knew that people who knew about it would know what it meant when it said "Love to turn you on," you kind of have a smoke, but there was such little reference that probably the only people who could understand it were people who were turned on anyway.

It was banned (by the BBC) on the basis of the line about how many holes does it take to fill the Albert Hall. Somebody got the idea it was how many holes there are in their arm. I think they heard it was something to do with drugs and that was the only part they could find that sounded like drugs. So that proved that the people who didn't know anything about drugs couldn't have been corrupted by it. "Turn you on" and "smoke" in normal language didn't mean anything. I suppose it might have corrupted a few people, but you can't really worry about that. We didn't at the time, anyway. We just thought, it'll be a nice in-joke for our friends.

Seeing that Let It Be *was released basically after the fact, do you wish it had not been released?*

Oh, no. I don't wish that about anything. Everything seems to take its place in history after it's happened and it's fine to let it stay there.

It was a Phil Spector salvage job, wasn't it?

Sort of. He was in with Allen Klein and Klein sort of brought him in. We had all lost interest, nobody was that interested in the record, so it was a bit of a salvage job for him. I was given a copy for approval and I rang up and found out he had already left and the album was coming out pretty much that way.

I'm not struck by the violins and ladies' voices on 'The Long and Winding Road.' I've always put my own strings on. But that's a bit of spilled milk. Nobody minded except me, so I shut up. When we first got it, Linda and I played it at home. It was a bit rough after *Abbey Road* had been very professional.

It was the first album to have little bits on, like the type that also appeared on 'McCartney'.

I rather fancied having just the plain tapes and nothing done to them at all. We had thought of doing something looser before, but the albums always turned out to be well-produced. That was the idea of the whole album. All the normal things that you record that are great and have all this atmosphere but aren't brilliant recordings or production jobs normally are left out and wind up on, say, Pete Townshend's cutting floor. It ends up with the rest of his demos.

But all that stuff is often stuff I love. It's got the door opening, the banging of the tape recorder, a couple of people giggling in the background. When you've got friends around, those are the kind of tracks you play them. You don't play them the big finished produced version.

Like 'Hey Jude,' I think I've got that tape somewhere, where I'm going on and on with all these funny words. I remember I played it to John and Yoko and I was saying, "these words won't be on the finished version." Some of the words were "the movement you need is on your shoulder", and John was saying, "It's great! 'The movement you need is on your shoulder.' " I'm saying "It's crazy, it doesn't make any sense at all." He's saying "Sure it does, it's great." I'm always saying that, by the way. That's me. I'm always never sure if it's good enough. That's me, you know.

So when *McCartney* came along I had all these rough things and I liked them all and thought, well, they're rough, but they've got that certain kind of thing about them, so we'll leave it and just put it out. It's not an album which was really sweated over, and yet now I find it's a lot of people's favourite. They think it's great to hear the kids screaming and the door opening. It's lovely.

In the back of everyone's mind there was always that kind of thing. The sound of a tape being spooled back is an interesting sound. If you're working in a recording studio, you hear it all the time and get used to it. You don't think anything of it. But when the man switches on the tape machine in the middle of a track and you hear that kind of "djeeoww", and then the track starts, I'd always liked all that, all those rough edges and loose ends. It gives a kind of live excitement.

When you do have rough edges on an album, you're open to interpretation. There's the

RETURN TO LIVERPOOL. AT THE TOWNHALL.

famous example of John and Yoko's 'Wedding Album, where the reviewer reviewed the tone on the test pressing and said that the subtle fluctuations in this tone were very arty.

The whole analysis business is a funny business, it's almost like creating history before it's been created. When a thing happens you immediately start analyzing it as if it was fifty years ago, as if it was King Henry VIII who said it. It is daft, actually, but you can't blame anyone for doing it, they've got to write something. Unless they can say "I was around at his house and he gave me a nice cup of tea . . . funny little blue cups he gave it in . . ." they've got to say, well, what did you mean by this, or what was that tone.

With one song you mentioned just a few minutes ago, 'Hey Jude,' everyone was trying to figure out who Jude was.

I happened to be driving out to see Cynthia Lennon. I think it was just after John and she had broken up, and I was quite mates with Julian (their son). He's a nice kid, Julian. And I was going out in me car just vaguely singing this song, and it was like "Hey, Jules." I don't know why, "Hey, Jules." It was just this thing, you know, "Don't make it bad/Take a sad song . . ." And then I just thought a better name was Jude. A bit more country and western for me.

In other words, it was just a name. It was just like "Hey Luke" or "Hey Max" or "Hey Abe", but "Hey Jude" was better. To one fellow Jude meant Jew, "Juden Raus," "Jew Get Out." At the time we had the Apple shop. I went in one night and put whitewash on all the windows and rubbed out 'Hey Jude' as a big ad. I thought it was a great thing, nothing happening in the shop, let's use the window as a big advertising thing for the record. So I did this 'Hey Jude' right across the window and some feller from a little Jewish delicatessen rang up the office the next day. He said "If my sons vere vif me, I'd sent von of them round to kill you. You are doing this terrible thing with the Jewish name. Wat you want, Juden Raus, you trying to start the whole Nazi thing again?"

Those are the kind of things, you know, that *do* happen. But really in nine cases out of ten, even when all this bit went down after the Beatles, John writing a song at me, me supposed to be writing songs back at him . . . OK, there was a little bit of it from my point of view, certain little lines, I'd be thinking, "Well, this will get him." You do, you know. Christ, you can't avoid it. 'Too Many People,' I wrote a little bit in that, "too many people preaching." That was actually the only thing I was saying referring to John at the time.

What I meant to say was, once you get analyzing something and looking into it, things *do* begin to appear and things *do* begin to tie in. Because *everything* ties in, and what you get depends on your approach to it. You look at everything with a black attitude and it's all black.

This other idea of Paul Is Dead. That was on for a while. I had just turned up at a photo

WITH JANE ASHER AT 'HOW I WON THE WAR' PERMIERE AND (INSET) PLAYING SHEA STADIUM.

FILMING 'HELP' ON SALISBURY PLAIN.

SUBTERRANEAN NEWS

also in this issue:
RUBIN ON CHICAGO
BURROUGHS ON WOODSTOCK
WEBERMAN ON DYLAN

25¢
35¢ OUTSIDE

OCT 29 1969

"It's High Time Our BILLY Received The Credit He Deserves" —— DAD

Paul's Lookalike Billy Shears

(Editors' note: Lee Merrick, an old friend of ours, sent this RAT exclusive by cable just a day before publication.)

by Lee Merrick

London—October 26. Paul McCartney is dead. All the Beatles, of course, know it but they aren't talking. All the insiders at Apple Corporation have known it for a long time without ever leaking a word. It's been the world's best-kept secret. But, in the last few days I have discovered absolute prrof of Paul's death; and I think it's time that the world knew the truth. The hoax has gone on long enough.

I have gotten to know a lot of people at Apple Corp. pretty well during the six months that I've hung around jamming and doing various studio gigs.

I had seen the Beatles, including 'Paul', many times around the studio and offices. Rumors about them are a dime a dozen. I had heard the one about Paul's death, but it was just one of scores that went around. Even when the death rumor received international press coverage, I didn't take the whole thing very seriously.

But my opinion changed radically as a result of a party I attended last Wednesday. The party, at the house of a London rock musician, included the usual assortment of hip writers, rocksters and hangers-on. Several Apple friends also showed up. The latest Beatle rumor was, of course, the main topic of conversation. Everyone there considered himself to be very in with the Beatles, and they all joked about the obvious foolishness of the latest outcropping of Beatlemania.

After a while, several of my Apple friends and I decided to split to one of their apartments to smoke a little dope and check out some new tapes that had just come in. People eventually drifted off to crash or ball, leaving only myself and my friend. I had noticed earlier that the light talk about Paul's rumored death had put him very up tight, and the idea to leave had been his in the first place. In the past few months we had grown pretty close—and we were pretty stoned—so I began to question him about the whole affair.

The story I drew out of him over the next few hours went like this:

Remember the first cut on the Sgt. Pepper album? The one with the line "And now we introduce to you the one and only Billy Shears"? Did you ever wonder just who 'Billy Shears' actually was? Of if he even existed?

Billy Shears was a young London rock musician who did short gigs in London nightclubs and occasional tours, waiting for the chance to make it big. As the fifties rock-and-roll craze spread across to Europe, he got a chance to play various clubs on the Continent. In 1962 Shears played on the same nightclub bill as Paul McCartney. In fact, he was virtually a dead ringer for Paul. Of course, you could tell the difference if they stood side by side. Billy had a somewhat over-sized, beak-shaped nose. But in photographs or at a distance, they were absolutely indistinguishable.

Their friendship remained intermittent over the next year or so as their respective tour paths occasionally crossed. When fame came to the Beatles in 1964, however, they lost touch with obscure Billy who drifted from small bandsman to studio musician.

In November, 1966, Paul McCartney was involved in an auto accident—a fatal accident. John, George and Ringo first wanted to stage a gigantic funeral in memory of Paul. But super-sharp manger, Brian Epstein, feared that Paul's death would destroy the Beatles mystique and managed almost entirely to suppress the news. Epstein's calculating mind had already devised a scheme for keeping the Beatles intact—at least for the public. With a minor nose job, Billy Shears would make a perfect replacement for Paul. Though hesitant at first, Shears soon accepted Epstein's offer. What musician could resist the opportunity to step into the shoes of one of *the* superstars of the rock world.

In the first album after Paul's death, Sgt. Pepper, the Beatles cryptically introduced the new "Paul" in the first cut. The album closes with "A Day in the Life", the story of Paul's death. (" . . . He blew his mind out in a car/He didn't notice that the light had changed/A crowd of people stood and stared/They'd seen his face before . . . ")

Knowing perhaps that the ruse couldn't last, the Beatles have hinted at the truth in every successive album. On the Sgt. Pepper album centerfold, only 'Paul' faces away from the camera; Epstein did not want a large close-up of 'Paul' to be shown until people became accustomed to the slight difference from the deceased Beatle. On the Magical Mystery Tour insert, only 'Paul' wears a black rose. "Revolution Number Nine", on the double album, contains the phrase "I buried Paul" when played backwards. The cover picture of the most recent Abbey Road shows the Beatles walking single file. The first two, Ringo and John, wear mourning clothes; 'Paul' is barefoot and dressed as for burial; George follows in the work clothes of an English gravedigger.

Even though I knew that my friend, who asked to remain un-named, had known and worked with the Beatles from the early days in the fifties, his story seemed almost too fantastic to believe. And certainly people who did not know him would have no reason to believe that Billy took Paul's place three years ago. So, for the next few days, I searched for evidence to absolutely confirm the story.

My search ended in the quiet Chelsea section of London where I talked with Philip Shears, father of the new Paul McCartney. At first, Mr. Shears hesitated to discuss the matter. He had kept his lips sealed for three long years in the pleasant, middle-class home his son had bought for him. But after I repeated the story my Apple friend had told me, the elderly Mr. Shears relented and confirmed the facts. "Mums and me always knew that it couldn't stay secret forever. The Beatles are a bunch of wonderful lads and have made a whole new world for us." But, he added, "It's high time that our Billy received the credit he deserves."

And now he has.

●●●●●●●●●●●●●

The Real Paul McCartney

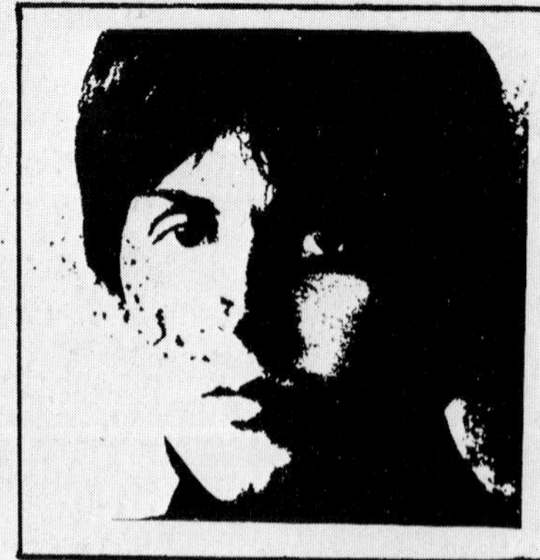

Billy Shears Before Cosmetic Surgery

TOKYO SOUVENIR SALESMAN, 1965.

session and it was at the time when Linda and I were just beginning to knock around with each other steadily. It was a hot day in London, a really nice hot day, and I think I wore sandals. I only had to walk around the corner to the crossing because I lived pretty nearby. I had me sandals on and for the photo session I thought I'd take my sandals off.

Linda: No, you *were* barefoot.

Oh, I was barefoot. Yeah, that's it. You know, so what? Barefoot, nice warm day, I didn't feel like wearing shoes. So I went around to the photo session and showed me bare feet. Of course when that came out and people start looking at it they say "Why has he got no shoes on? He's never done *that* before." OK, you've never seen me do it before, but in actual fact, it's just me with my shoes off. Turns out to be some old Mafia sign of death or something.

Then the this-little-bit-if-you-play-it- backwards stuff. As I say, nine times out of ten it's really nothing. Take the end of 'Sergeant Pepper', that backwards thing. "We'll fuck you like Supermen." Some fans came around to my door giggling. I said, "Hello, what do you want?" They said, "Is it true, that bit at the end? Is it true? It says 'We'll fuck you like Supermen.' " I said, "No, you're kidding. I haven't heard it, but I'll play it." It was just some piece of conversation that was recorded and turned backwards. But I went inside after I'd seen them and played it seriously, turned it backwards with my thumb against the motor, turned the motor off and did it backwards. And there it was, sure as anything, plain as anything. "We'll fuck you like Supermen." I thought, Jesus, what can you do?

And then there was "I buried Paul."

That wasn't "I buried Paul" at all, that was John saying "cranberry sauce." It was the end of 'Strawberry Fields Forever.' That's John's humor. John would say something totally out of synch, like "cranberry sauce." If you don't realize that John's apt to say "cranberry sauce" when he feels like it, then you start to hear a funny little word there, and you think "Aha!"

When you were alive and presumed dead, what did you think?

Someone from the office rang me up and said "Look, Paul, you're dead." And I said, "Oh, I don't agree with that." And they said, "Look, what are you going to do about it? It's a big thing breaking in America. You're dead." And so I said leave it, just let them say it. It'll probably be the best publicity we've ever had and I won't have to do a thing except stay alive. So I managed to stay alive through it.

A couple of people came up and said "Can I photograph you to prove you're not dead?" Coincidentally, around about that time, I was playing down a lot of the old Beatle image and getting a bit more to what I felt was me, letting me beard grow and not being so hung up on keeping fresh and clean. I *looked* different, more laid back, and so I had people coming up saying "You're not him!" And I was beginning to think, "I am, you know, but I know what you mean. I

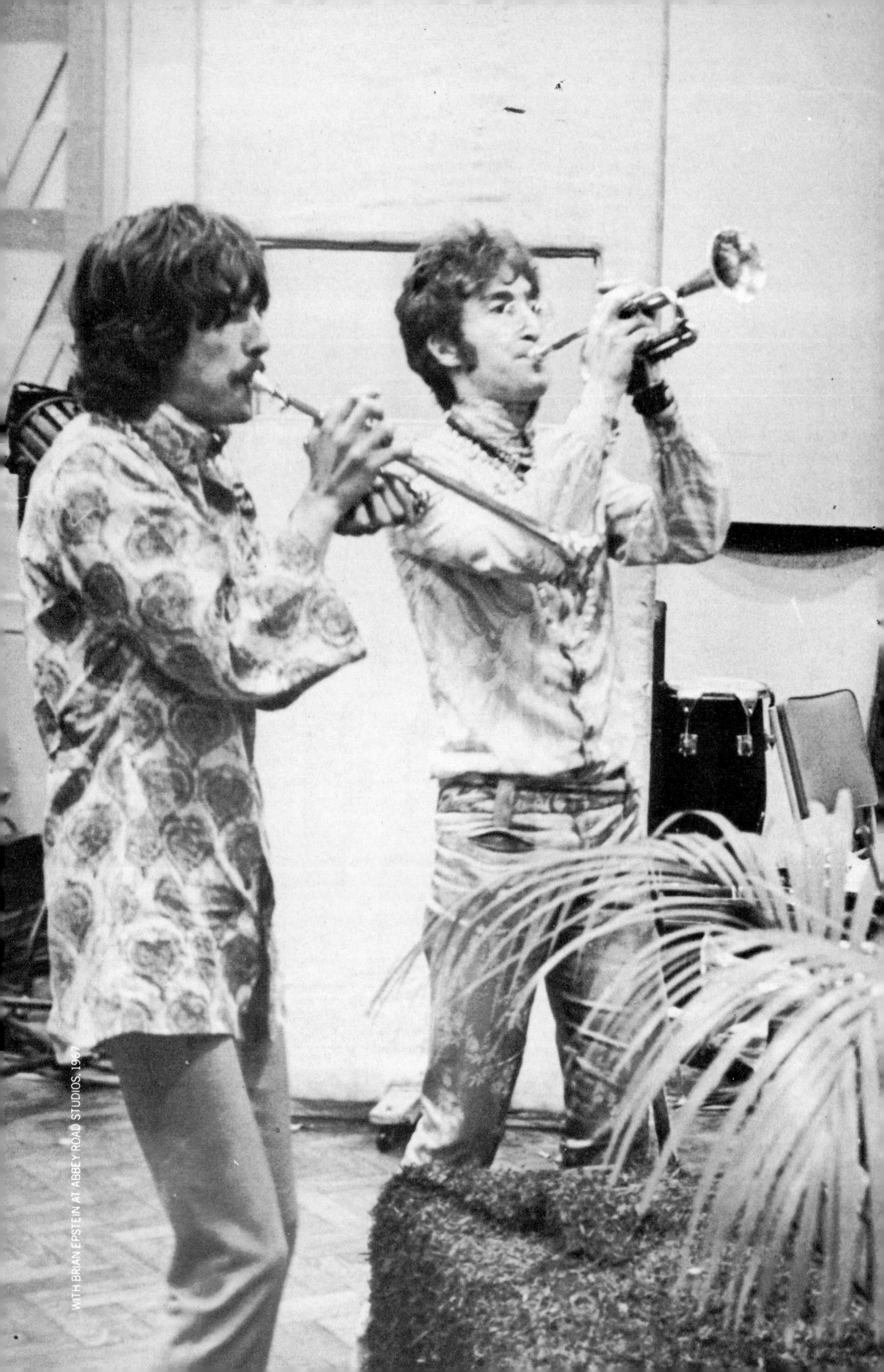

WITH BRIAN EPSTEIN AT ABBEY ROAD STUDIOS, 1967

don't *look* like him, but believe me."

You were supposedly Billy Shears, according to one of the theories.

Ringo's Billy Shears. Definitely. That was just in the production of *Sergeant Pepper.* It just happened to turn out that we dreamed up Billy Shears. It was a rhyme for "years" . . . "band you've know for all these years . . . and here he is, the one and only Billy Shears." We thought, that's a great little name, it's an Eleanor-Rigby-type name, a nice atmospheric name, and it was leading into Ringo's track. So as far as we were concerned it was purely and simply a device to get the next song in.

In the film 'A Hard Day's Night' there were the stereotypes – if you remember John the thinker, Ringo the loner, Paul the happy-go-lucky. Did you object to that?

No, I didn't mind it. No, no; I still don't. I was in a film. I don't care what they picture me as. So far as I'm concerned I'm just doing a job in a film. If the film calls for me to be a cheerful chap, well, great; I'll be a cheerful chap.

It does seem to have fallen in my role to be kind of a bit more that than others. I was always known in the Beatle thing as being the one who would kind of sit the press down and say, "Hello, how are you? Do you want a drink?" and make them comfortable. I guess that's me. My family loop was like that. So I kind of used to do that, plus a little more polished than I might normally have done, but you're aware you're talking to the press . . . You want a good article, don't you, so you don't want to go slagging the guys off.

But I'm not ashamed of anything I've been, you know. I kind of like the idea of doing something and if it turns out in a few years to look a bit sloppy I'd say "Oh, well, sloppy. So what?" I think most people dig it. You get people living in Queens or say Red Creek, Minnesota, and they're all wiped out themselves . . . you know, ordinary people. Once you get into the kind of critical bit, people analyzing you and then you start to analyze yourself, and you think, oh Christ, you got me, and things start to rebound on you, why didn't I put on a kind of smart image . . . you know, why wasn't I kind of tougher? I'm not really tough. I'm not really lovable, either, but I don't mind falling in the middle. My dad's advice: moderation, son. Every father in the world tells you moderation. (Linda laughs hysterically in the background.)

British parents aren't different . . .

No, they're exactly the same. My dad could be the perfect American stereotype father. He's a good lad, though. I like him, you know.

I tell you what. I think that a lot of people worried about that kind of stuff often didn't have very good family scenes, and something happened in their family to make them bitter. OK, in the normal day-to-day life a lot of polished talk goes on . . . you don't love everyone you meet, but you try and get on with people, you know, you don't try and put 'em uptight; most people don't, anyway.

So to me that's always been the way. I mean, there's nothing wrong with that. Why should I go around slagging people? I really didn't like all that John did. But I'm sure that *he* doesn't now.

Have you talked to him about that?

No, but I know John and I know that most of it was just something to tell the newspapers. He was in that mood then and he wanted all that to be said. I think now, whilst he probably doesn't *regret* it, he didn't mean every single syllable of it. I mean, he came out with all stuff like I'm like Engelbert Humperdinck. I know he doesn't *really* think that. In the press, they really wanted me to come out and slam John back and I used to get pissed off at the guys coming up to me and saying, "This is the latest thing John said and what's your answer?" You know, really limp things, I'd answer. But I believe keep cool and that sort of thing, and it passes over. I don't believe if someone kind of punches you over you have to go kind of thumping him back to prove you're a man and that kind of thing. I think, actually, you do win that way in the end.

What was your reaction when you read that stuff at the time?

Oh, I hated it. You can imagine, I sat down and pored over every little paragraph, every little sentence. "Does he really think that of me?" I thought. And at the time I thought, "It's me. I am. That's just what I'm like. He's captured me so well; I'm a turd, you know." I sat down and really thought, I'm just nothing. But then, people who dug me like Linda said "Now you know that's not true, you're joking. He's got a grudge, man; the guy's trying to polish you off." Gradually I started to think, great, that's not true. I'm not really like Engelbert; I don't just write ballads. And that kept me hanging on; but at the time, I tell you, it hurt me. Whew. Deep.

Could you write a song or songs with John again?

Anything could happen. I like to write with John. I like to write with anyone who's good.

The Wings tour in 1972 was the first time you had toured in six years, wasn't it?

Yes.

Had you intended to keep it that long?

Oh, no, no, no. With the Beatles we did a big American tour, and I think the feeling, mainly from George and John, was, "Oh, this is getting a little bit *uhhh* . . . But I thought, "No, you can't give up live playing, we'd be crazy to."

But then we did a concert tour I really hated and I came off stormy and saying "Bloody hell, I really agree with you now."

Where was that?

In America, somewhere, I can't remember exactly. It was raining and we were playing under some sort of big canopy and everybody felt they were going to get electric shocks and stuff. We were driven off in a big truck afterwards and I remember sitting in the back of the truck saying, bloody hell, they're right, this is stupid.

So we knew we were going to give up playing but we didn't want to go make some big

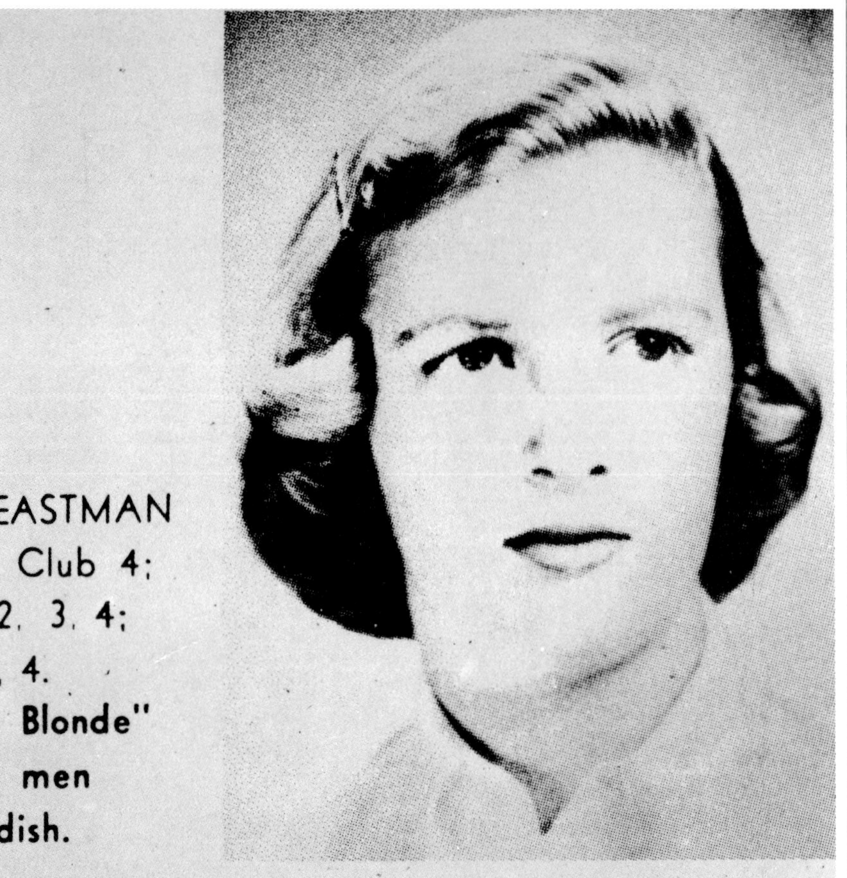

FROM SCARSDALE HIGHSCHOOL YEARBOOK.

announcement, that we were giving it all up or anything, so we just kind of cooled it and didn't go out. When anyone asked we'd say "Oh, we'll be going out again," but we really didn't think we would. So we recorded a lot of stuff and nobody felt the need to go out and play.

I remember at the end of the Beatles thinking that it would be good if I just went out with some country and western group. To have a sing every day surely must improve my voice a bit. Live shows are a lot of what it's all about. If nothing else, you get out there . . .

At your Oxford press conference you mentioned your four-year-old daughter liked the Osmonds. Linda says your ten-year-old daughter is a bit off them now . . .

Yes, she is a bit . . .

. . . but I understand you met the Osmonds in Paris, which is a very unusual situation. It must have been as much of a thrill for them to meet you as it would be for a four-year-old to meet them.

A layer cake of generations.

As we're talking today three of the Top Six here (England) are by them, which is the greatest chart domination by a group since 1964.

They're very liked here by a lot of the record buyers, who in Britain are the young kids.

From your personal experience, do you think they can understand how much they mean to people?

Sure they know, sure. I think Little Jimmy probably knows less than the others what's going on, but they seem to. They've got that kind of American showbiz family feeling, which does work. You can put it down, but it really does work. They've been doing it for years on *The Andy Williams Show,* and they're troupers already. You know, the kid's only eight or something, Little Jimmy, but he's already a little trouper. He has what a seasoned performer has.

When you were in their position, did you feel a sense of responsibility, or did you feel the world had gone crazy?

No, no. We were a band who'd been trying to make it big for a long time. When you're trying to get to the top, when you start to get there, that's probably the biggest thrill. You don't think the whole world's gone crazy; you think it's great that they like you and you're well-chuffed that you're going down so well. That's all that enters your head. I think that even Little Jimmy just thinks, "Hey, man, that's great, that's far out." You know? He just loves it. And that's really the best way.

When you get thinking too heavily about all of this stuff, like anything, you can do so many double thinks on it all you end up with is not liking it, which is the only hang-up. When you end up not liking it then you start to do it less well. I always thought, just great, great band, great things, kids screaming, fantastic, fabulous,

WEDDING PHOTOGRAPH OUTSIDE THEIR ST. JOHN'S WOOD HOME WITH MAL EVANS AND McCARTNEY MANAGER PETER BROWN.

BATHING DAUGHTER MARY AT HOME AND (INSET) RECORDING 'LET IT BE' WITH LINDA'S DAUGHTER HEATHER.

great, everyone's having a good night out. That sort of thing, basically.

Now that you have your US visa, I suppose the rumours will start again. There'll be a Beatles reunion of some sort?

Well, I must say, like as far as getting together as we were, as the Beatles were, I don't thing that'll ever happen again. I think now everyone's kind of interested in their little personal things. I like the way we did 'Band on the Run.'

But I do think that I for one am very proud – although I don't like the word proud, it tends to be . . . ex-servicemen have used the word, if you know what I mean . . . "proud of my country" . . . but I will use the word – I am proud of the Beatle thing. It was great and I can go along with all the people you meet on the street who say you gave so much happiness to many people. I don't think that's corny. At the time obviously it just passes over; you don't really think they mean it. Oh yeah, sure, and you shake their hand or whatever.

But I dig all that like mad now, and I believe that we did bring a real lot of happiness to the times. So I'm very proud of that kind of stuff and consequently I wouldn't like to see my past slagged off. So I would like to see more co-operation . . . if things go right, if things keep cool, I'd like to maybe do some work with them; I've got a lot of ideas in my head, but I wouldn't like to tell you before I tell them. We couldn't be the Beatles-back-together-again, but there might be things, little good ventures we could get together on, mutually helpful to all of us and things people would like to see, anyway.

I wouldn't rule everything out, it's one of those questions I really have to hedge on. But, I mean, I'm ready. Once we settle our business crap – there was an awful lot of money made, of course, and none of it came to use, really, in the end. Virtually, that's the story. So I'd kind of like to salvage some of that and see that not everything's ripped off.

Through all the bitterness I tended to think like John a bit. "Oh, the Beatles . . . naww . . . Crap." But it really wasn't. I think it was great. So I'd like to see that cooled out and restored to its kind of former greatness, agree that it was a good thing and continue in some kind of way. I don't see gettin' the Beatles back together – there's certain things we could do quite quietly and still produce some kind of ongoing thing. I don't think you'll ever get anyone to give up all their individual stuff now; everyone's got it going too well now.

Would you consider the Ringo *album an example of that kind of cooperation?*

Yeah, but I think more than that. I think that's a beginning. That shows what someone can do just if he asks. That's all he did. He just asked us all. So that's what I like, no one says, "Naw, you go on and make your own album." So if it's that easy then lots of things could be done in the future. And I'd like to see some great things done.

THE ROT OF APPLE: SUE ME, SUE YOU.

In America, the anthology album (Beatles 1967-70) *and* Red Rose Speedway *were back-to-back Number Ones. You were replacing yourself. Did that strike you as odd?*

I thought it was good, rather than odd, because obviously the big hang up after the Beatles broke up was, and really still is, can any of them be as good as the unit? The answer in most people's minds, I think, is "No, they can't." Because the unit was *so* good.

Were you glad those anthology albums were released for the historical record or to combat the bootleggers?

The bootlegging thing was one of the reasons. I didn't take an awful lot of interest in them, actually. I still haven't heard them. I know what's on them because I've heard it all before, you know. I haven't really taken much interest in Beatles stuff of late just because there has been this hangover of Apple and Klein. The whole scene has gone so bloody sick. The four ex-Beatles are totally up to here with it. Everyone wants it solved so everyone can get on with being a bit peaceful with each other.

There was a lawsuit recently, the three others against Klein.

Of course I loved that. My God, I hope they win that one. That's great. You see, apart from everything that came down, all the little personal conflicts, the reason why I felt I had to do what I had to do, which ended up specifically as being I had to sue the other three, was that there was no way I could sue Klein on his own, which is what I wanted to do. It took me months to get over the fact. I kept saying, I can't sue the other three, just because it's very hard news to go suing someone you like, and no matter what kind of personal things were going down and John writing songs about me and all that stuff, I still didn't feel the coolest thing in the world was to go and sue them. But it actually turned out to be the only way to stop Klein, so I had to go and do it.

Then it all started to come out, you know, that Klein had persuaded George – I don't know how much of this is libelous –

Our lawyers will take out whatever is libellous.

Klein made his way into George's big songwriting company, which is George's big asset. The main one was the song "Something," that was on *Abbey Road.* That was kind of George's great big song, George's first big effort, and everyone covered it and it was lovely and made him lots of money that he could give away, which is his thing, you know. It was a great thing for him. Well, it turns out that Klein has got himself into that company. Not only paid 20% (the percentage Klein claimed to have gotten from *Abbey Road*) – there's a thought now that he's claiming he owns the company!

It's those kinds of little weird trips. Now the only good thing I feel is that I wasn't wrong. I would have felt really bad if I was wrong and the guy was really a goodie all along and I'd gone and stuck my big nose in there like the pot calling the kettle black. But it turns out he is the type of man who wants to own it for himself and not the type of man who believes the artist should have it and do what he wants with it, which is what I believe.

He was once quoted in New York magazine as saying he was going to roast your ass.

Yeah, well, he never did, you know, and that's cool. He wouldn't get near my ass to roast it, anyway. Punk.

You mentioned you had to sue the other three to get at Klein. What was Klein doing that made you have to sue?

IN APPLE'S SAVILLE ROW OFFICES AND (INSET) WITH YOKO ONO AND JOHN LENNON.

Basically, I was being held to my obligations under an old contract. I would have to just sit, lump it, and let him be my manager, which I didn't want.

So I was told I could sue him. I said, "Great, I'll sue him." Then they said, "There's one catch, you have to sue Apple" – and that meant suing the other three. For two months I sat around thinking, "I can't do this." Not that I didn't see the others. I did, and kept asking them to let me out and they said, "No, Allen says there would be tax complications." I said, "I don't give a damn about tax considerations, let me go and I'll worry about the tax considerations. I don't want to be an ABKCO-Managed Industry." It was weird, my albums would come out saying "An ABKCO Company." and he wasn't even my manager.

As it turns out, it was the best thing, because that got the receiver in there and froze the money and gave everybody time to think about it. He's still managed to get $5 million transferred to his own company, five million for management (exact amount subject matter of litigation).

He has a very special gift for talking his way. He'll use his *Playboy* interviews, and he'll probably ask for a *Rolling Stone* interview after mine. Even a murderer has a great line in his own defence. But he's nothing more than a trained New York crook. John said, "Anyone whose record is as bad as this can't be so bad." But that was Lennonesque crap, which John occasionally did; utter foolishness. Klein had already been convicted on ten counts of income tax. (Criminal docket 66–72 of US District Court, Southern

(INSET) WITH THE MAHARISHI IN NORTH WALES, 1967.

RECORDING A TV THEME WITH THE BLACK DYKE MILLS BAND AND (INSET) WITH AN AMERICAN FAN AT APPLE'S OFFICES.

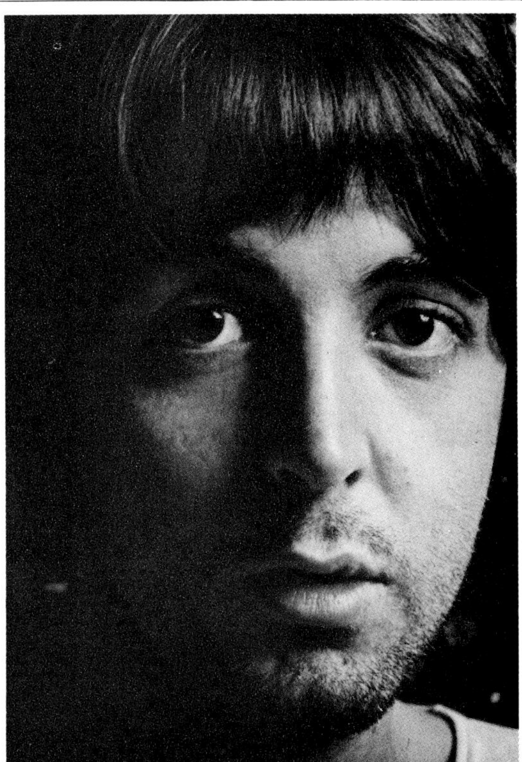

District of New York, shows one Allen Klein found guilty January 29th, 1971, on ten counts of "unlawfully failing to make and file returns of Federal income taxes and FICA taxes withheld from employees' wages." Conviction affirmed on appeal by US Court of Appeals for the Second Circuit November 19th, 1971). My back was against the wall. I'm not proud of it. But it had to be done. To him, artists are money. To me, they're more than that.

If Klein was the big reason for the breakup of Apple, do you think there would have been difficulties anyway without him?

I think there would have been difficulties. Had the Eastmans come in like I wanted, the others would have feared I was trying to screw everyone for the Eastmans. It would have been a bit hard for the others to swallow, I'm afraid, since the Eastmans were so close to me. But they didn't want to screw anybody, and the way it's turning out they're settling up most of it anyway. Some people say, "People are all the same in business," but they're not.

In thinking of James Taylor and some of the other Apple artists, do you think Apple turned out to be a good idea for them?

I think the Apple thing was great. As it turned out, the one thing about business is that it does have to be looked after. If you have paperwork and bills and royalties and accounts and stuff, they all have to be handled very well, or else things get lost and then accountants have great difficulty in making up the final picture for taxes.

Apple was together in a lot of other ways. Although he didn't get treated brilliantly at

Apple, it was right for James Taylor to make his first record then. I think it was shameful of them to sue him afterwards, but I think that was largely Klein's instigation because of the way he works. He's kind of, "OK, let's git the bastard. He's left us and he's a success, let's sue him. We got him, we got his contract."

But I still think all the records that came out of it, Billy Preston and James Taylor, Badfinger, Mary Hopkin, all the people we did take on all had very good records. George, even with the Radha Krishna Temple, I think that's great stuff. I don't think you can fault any of the artistic decisions. Looking back on it I think it was really a very successful thing.

The main downfall is that we were less businessmen and more heads, which was very pleasant and very enjoyable, except there should have been the man in there who would tell us to sign bits of paper. We got a man in who started to say, come on, sign it all over to me, which was the fatal mistake.

Just as I was going to do a radio show interview the other day, just as I was walking in, this feller walked up to me and said, "Hello, Paul," and I thought I'd seen him somewhere before. He looked kind of middle-aged, 50ish, and I thought, "What's he want with me? Looks a bit dubious." He pushed a little bit of paper in me hand, he said, "I don't want to embarrass you, Paul, I'm sure you know what this is all about, but I've got my job to do." A wife and three kids, all that. So I walked on, muttering, looked at the bit of paper and it says "ABKCO hereby sue you, John, George and Ringo and everything you've ever been connected with," in so many words, companies I'd never even heard of. "Sue you all for the sum of $20 million." That is the latest little line.

I'm not trying to be immodest by classing myself with Van Gogh or with the biggies in the artistic world, but it is just a pure continuation of that kind of story. The whole idea of whoever makes the thing not being given the profits of it isn't a new idea. I think it's a joke, trying to sue us for that amount of money. It is just purely that he thinks, in some way, that he owns us. The laugh is that on that whole Klein thing there is one key thing which I luckily would never sign, so I feel a little bit out of that one, I must say.

Linda mentioned Lew Grade's claim that she couldn't write.

That was an old one. Around that time we had millions of suits flying here, flying there, George wrote the 'Sue Me, Sue You Blues' about it. I'd kicked it all off originally, having to sue the other three Beatles in the High Court, and that opened Pandora's box. After that everybody just seemed to be suing everybody.

Meanwhile Lew Grade suddenly saw his song-writing concessions, which he'd just paid an awful lot of money for, virtually to get hold of John and I, he suddenly saw that I was now claiming that I was writing half my stuff with Linda, and that if I was writing half of it she was

DURING THE RECORDING OF 'LET IT BE' WITH STEP-DAUGHTER HEATHER.

entitled to a pure half of it, no matter whether she was a recognized songwriter or not. I didn't think that was important, I thought that whoever I worked with, no matter what the method of collaboration was, that person, if they did help me on the song, should have a portion of the song for helping me. I think at the time their big organization suddenly thought, "Hello, they're pulling a fast one, they're trying to get some of the money back," whereas in fact, it was the truth. So they slapped vast amounts on us, I can't remember what.

I wrote Sir Lew Grade a long letter saying, "Don't you think I ought to be able to do this and do that and don't you think I've done enough and don't you think I'm OK and – Hey, man, why have you gotta sue me?" He wrote me back a very rational letter. I can't remember exactly what it said, but it was a very nice letter. He's actually OK, Lew, he's all right.

You did a TV show for him (James Paul McCartney).

After it, yeah, that's right. All the suits were dropped by then. (Bites his tongue).

Your two big television shows were James Paul McCartney *and* Magical Mystery Tour. *How were these conceived?*

The Mystery show was conceived way back in Los Angeles. On the plane. You know they give you those big menus and I had a pen and everything and started drawing on this menu and

STILL FROM TV SHOW 'JAMES PAUL McCARTNEY'

I had this idea. In England they have these things called Mystery tours. And you go on them and you pay so much and you don't know where you're going. So the idea was to have this little thing advertised in the shop windows somewhere called Magical Mystery Tours. Someone goes in and buys a ticket and rather than just being the kind of normal publicity type of magical . . . well, it never was magical, really . . . the idea of the show was that it was actually a magical run . . . a real magical trip.

I did a few little sketches myself and everyone else thought up a couple of little things. John thought of a little thing and George thought of a scene and we just kind of built it up. Then we hired a coach and picked actors out of an actor's directory and we just got them all along with the coach and we said, "OK, act." An off-the-cuff kind of thing.

The *James Paul McCartney* show were these people who wanted us to do a TV show and they said they wanted a nice show and said you can do it anyway you want. This seemed like a good opportunity, you know, to kinda get on the telly. So that one was just worked up that way. We met the guy when we went to Morocco. We were on holiday then and they came out and sat around the pool and talked about various ideas and came back to England and did it.

Were you sorry Magical Mystery Tour *was not shown in America?*

At the time, hey, I thought, "Oh, blimey," but . . . eh . . . it started out to be one of those kind of things like *The Wild One,* you know, Marlon Brando . . . at the time it couldn't be released. The interest in it came later. The interest started to grow, you know. *Magical Mystery Tour* was a bit like that . . . well, whatever happened to it . . . that's a bit magical itself. Like the Stones' *Rock and Roll Circus.* You know, what happened to that, you know. I mean, I'd like to see that. So all of those things work out well. You've got to be patient. Everything like that works out well. I think it was a good show. It will have its day, you know.

There was an interesting reaction to James Paul McCartney. *Some people liked some parts and didn't like others.*

I can understand that. You know, I think a lot of people thought we could have done more . . . could have done a better show. It was a little bitty (a British expression for "disjointed"). That was a fair comment, but I got a lot of letters from people, you know, just people, old people, from like Red Creek, Minnesota, just saying "Hey man, dug the show, you know."

Had George (Harrison) invited you to the Bangla Desh benefit?

George invited me, and I must say it was more than just visa problems. At the time there was the whole Apple thing. When the Beatles broke up, at first I thought, "Right, broken up, no more messing with any of that." George came up and asked if I wanted to play Bangla Desh and I thought, blimey, what's the point? We've just broken up and we're joining up again! It just seemed a bit crazy.

There were a lot of things that went down then, most of which I've forgotten now. I really felt annoyed – "I'm not going to do that if he won't bloody let me out of my contract." Something like that. For years there had been problems as to why the other three felt they couldn't just rip up our partnership agreement. I thought it was crazy if we had split up as a band to have this piece of paper still going on. We were all tied into it and I wanted to break it up and they said "Tax, you can't." Klein was saying, "You can't do it, lads, you've got to stay together," and I think I know why he was saying it. He was telling the others it was tax and it was impossible and stuff.

There was an awful lot of that, and a lot of what I did around then was just out of bitterness at all that. I thought, "This is crazy, no one likes me enough to just let me go, give me my little bit of the proceeds and let me split off." It was a little tit-for-tat, if you're not going to do this for me, I'm not going to do that for you. I tend to see the others now just for the business. It's a bit daft, actually. That's why I'm so hot to get these business things over with.

Lee (Eastman) said the show you'll do for Phoenix House as part of the arrangement for your visa will be part of a tour.

The only thing now, obviously, is that it's dependent on getting a band together. The Phoenix House people helped to get me in. It's a good cause. We just went down to see one of their branches in East Harlem, just now. It's fantastic. I wasn't thinking it would be much, I thought it would be a bit depressing. But it's a beautiful place. There's a lot of love in that place. And it's not the kind of a state thing. There's discipline, too, but the discipline comes out of love. That way no one minds the discipline. If you just start off with discipline and nothing else, a lot of the kids find it hard to do it. But they're all very self-supporting now. It's a great place, I must say. Anyone who's in trouble with drugs, pills, junk, or whatever, should take a look in the Phoenix House.

What was the reaction of the kids when you went in there?

Great. We just shook hands. Their choir sang some songs and we went on a little tour of the house. There was a guy telling us about encounter meetings, how he was putting the bathroom in, doing all the plumbing himself – they're all very proud, because they're all people who almost messed up. They just made it, and most of them look like they can really go on to great strength because of it.

Would you like America to be a big proper tour or small, like your university tour?

A big proper tour. I think if you're coming to the States, you can't do it funky. I don't think I could, anyway. I think now I'll be ready to do a big concert tour, although I find it hard to imagine at the moment.

ON THE FARM IN SCOTLAND PHOTOGRAPHED BY LINDA.

LIFE WITH THE FAMILY: MR. & MRS. McCARTNEY

Linda and I met in a club in London called the Bag o' Nails, which was right about the time that the club scene was going strong in London. She was down there with some friends. I think she was down there with Chas Chandler and some other people, and I was down there with some friends, including a guy who used to work at the office. I was in my little booth and she was in her little booth and we were giving each other the eye, you know. Georgie Fame was playing that night and we were both right into Georgie Fame.

When did you first realize you wanted to marry her?

About a year later. We both thought it a bit crazy at the time, and we also thought it would be a gas. Linda was a bit dubious, because she had been married before and wasn't too set on settling. In a way, she thought it tends to blow up things, marrying ruins it. But we both fancied each other enough to do it. And now we're glad we did it, you know. It's great. I love it.

Some of the critical notices on her debut performances seemed to ask where she had come from.

Yeah. Well, the answer is, nowhere, really.

Mick Jagger had that quote. He wouldn't let . . .

. . . his old lady in the band, yeah. That was all very understandable at the time because she did kind of appear out of nowhere. To most people, she was just some chick. I just figure she was the main help for me on the albums around that time. She was there, every day, helping on harmonies and all that stuff.

It's like when you write millions of love songs and finally when you're in love you'd like to write one for the person you're in love with. So I think all this business about getting Linda in the billing was just a way of saying, "Listen, I don't care what you think, this is what I think. I'm putting her right up here with me."

Later we thought it might have been cooler not to introduce her so bluntly. Perhaps a little more show business: "Ladies and gentlemen, I'd like to introduce you to my better half. Isn't she sweet and coy?"

It turns out it didn't matter, it didn't matter one bit. At the time it was a little tough, maybe. At the time it was rough for her. None of us realized what . . . it was like someone marrying Mick, you don't realize . . . you *know* there's going to be a lot of fans who are going to hate it, but you still end up thinking, well, it's my life. I know of a lot of rock and roll stars or even just show business people who will regulate their life to their image. It can mess you up a lot. I know a lot of guys from the old days who wouldn't get married, even if they wanted to. Wouldn't get married because it might affect their careers. The old management thing – "You can't get married, all your fans are going to desert you." So the guy doesn't get married.

But the thing is, in a couple of years, his career is over anyway. And he didn't get married, and he went and blew it. So I didn't. "Well, I'm not going to let that kind of thing interfere with *me.*" Although I didn't wish to blow my career, I thought it was more important to get on with living. We went ahead and just did what we felt like doing. Some of it came out possibly a bit offensive to some people, but it turns out that it didn't matter in the first place. You just keep going.

Did your friends in music stick by you at that time or did you find it a little tough? Or did you have that many friends at the time?

I remember Ringo saying at the time "How many friends have I got?" and he couldn't count

TWO PHOTOS, BOTH TAKEN BY PAUL, AFTER BIRTH OF MARY McCARTNEY.

them on one hand. And that's what it boils down to, really. You can have millions of friends, but when someone asks you how many friends you've got, it depends on how honestly you're going to answer. Because I don't think I have that many. No one went against me or anything, I just isolated myself a bit. It's just one of those things. We had just met for the first time. We're very romantic, the both of us, and we didn't really want to hang out with anyone else.

Do you often go back to Liverpool?

We visit to keep in touch with the Liverpool scene. My family roots are up there, our kids love it, and my brother still lives there. In fact, we're going to make an album with him in January.

Will it come out as a Mike McGear album?

That's right. It's a singing thing, he's quit comedy for the moment. We're going to do it at Strawberry Studios in Stockport. We'll play it by ear, it's Mike's album.

Is it difficult for the kids, being your daughters?

I don't think so, I don't think they're going to be crazed-out kids. But it is funny sometimes. I remember I was sitting in a field and Heather was leading Mary and little baby on a pony, and Mary just said to me, "You're Paul McCartney, aren't you?" When she's talking to me normally, she'll just call me Daddy. When there's company around, she knows I'm Paul McCartney, in inverted commas.

It's nice that we have all girls. If we had a son it might be harder on him, like Frank Sinatra, Jr. Everyone assumes he'll turn out to be his dad. At the moment, there's not much to worry about with the kids.

Did you feel scared when McCartney *was released, since that was your debut and the first song was pegged at you?*

Linda: No. I didn't take it as seriously as I probably should have. I think it was good copy at the time to slag everything. Everybody was getting slagged, the Beatles were getting slagged. I personally didn't realize you had to explain yourself a lot once you get in the public eye. I just carried on with my normal life, like I had in New York, and I just got all this slagging. It never really brought me down much, though.

Do you think any Mrs. McCartney in that situation would have been slagged?

Linda: I think in what was going down then, yes. There was so much trouble for everybody, not done by one particular person, that everybody was getting blamed. I still can't look at it from the angle that I'm Mrs. McCartney. You know what I mean? I still see me as the person I've always been, either you like me or you don't. Paul likes me. (Laughter).

And stood up for you during the slagging.

Linda: He was living with me, he knows I'm a good chick, he knows I don't have any bad motives. I'm not a grabber, I'm not any of that. He wouldn't have married me if I had been. So he stuck by me.

I just read totally bizarre stuff about myself. People would do an article on me and then an

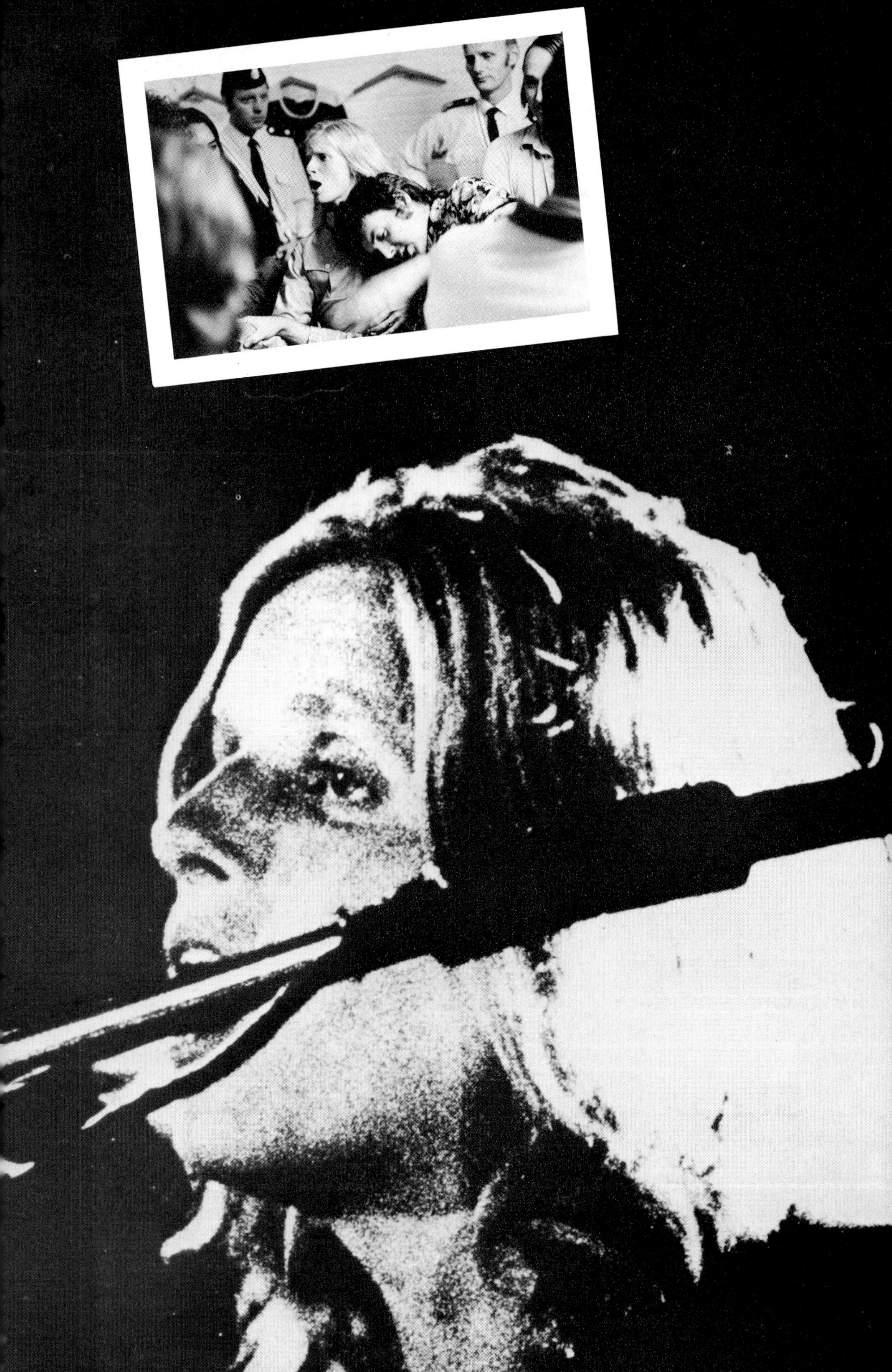

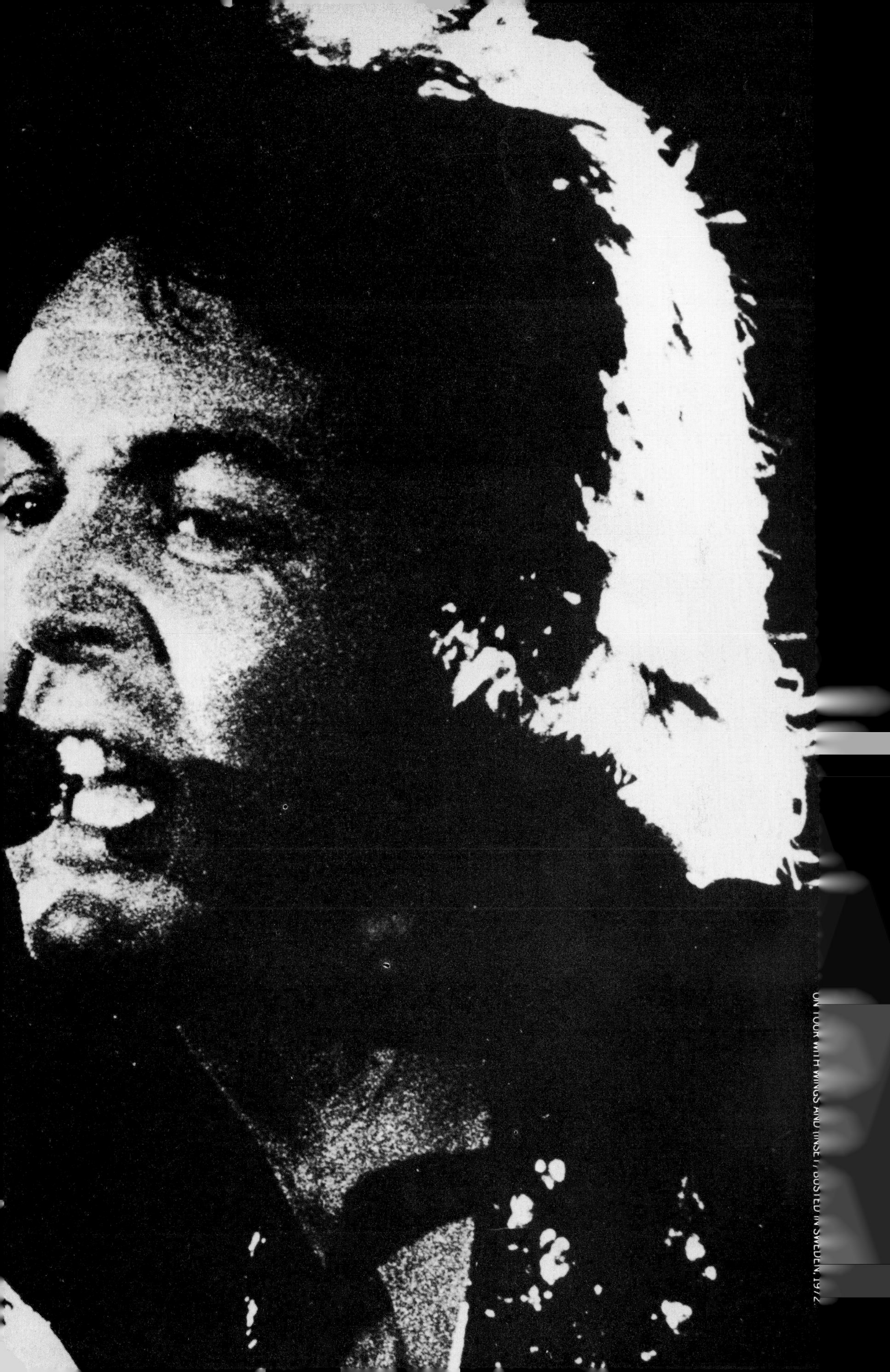

ON TOUR WITH WINGS AND INSET, BUSTED IN SWEDEN, 1972.

ON THE FARM IN SCOTLAND WITH NEW-BORN MARY.

article on Yoko from childhood on up. I couldn't believe it. It was total fantasy. I mean, none of that happened, folks.

Unlike John, who went to a solo career, Paul went to a group.

Linda: John didn't really go to a solo career, there was the Plastic Ono Band and that. But Paul *is* very much a teamwork person. He doesn't like working just on his own. He still gets nervous. He likes working with people, bouncing off people and having them bounce off him. He likes helping people.

Have you ever entertained the thought of doing a record by yourself?

Linda: Not Linda McCartney's Great Single, no. I fool around with the songs I write, but I don't take it as a serious career.

You do have the novelty single coming up?

Linda: Yes. I did a song, 'Seaside Woman,' right after we'd been to Jamaica, about three or four years ago, I guess. Very reggae-inspired. That's when ATV was suing us saying I was incapable of writing, so Paul said, "Get out and write a song." And then about a week ago we went in to a B side for it of something I'd written in Africa, and we just talk over it. It's very sort of Fifties R&B, the Doves, the Penguins. I love that, that was my era. I'm New York, you know, Alan Freed and the whole bit.

We're going to put the single out under the name Suzi and the Red Stripes. When we were in Jamaica, there had been a fantastic reggae version of 'Suzi Q,' so they used to call me Suzi. And the beer in Jamaica is called Red Stripe, so that makes it Suzi and the Red Stripes. It'll be out someday, but I've been saying 'Seaside Woman' will be released since 1971 and we still haven't bothered. It's a bit like my photography book. Someday there *will* be a book.

Was it strictly through you that your father became associated with Paul as his lawyer?

Linda: It's through me, actually. I remember saying to my father, when I'd met Paul a few times but wasn't living with him, after Brian died, that he helped a lot of people out of messes, could he help? He said well, I don't know. I said it would be great because I know you could help them out. So then I introduced Paul to my dad, and they got along instantly. If he hadn't met my father, Klein would have just hawked in there.

(At this point we retire to the control room. Linda goes over the Walt Disney Christmas Show script; Linda and Paul are to co-host the BBC holiday special. She talks on the phone to someone at EMI. "I think the only bit we'd like to add is a little bit from '101 Dalmations'. . ."

Paul talks to Alan Parsons, engineer of *Dark Side of the Moon.* They marvel at its sales record, and the engineer notes that Pink Floyd are going to give him a Christmas present. "Ask for a percentage," McCartney recommends. "It's the best present they could give you. What that album has done so far is amazing. In France it's outsold *Abbey Road*. . .")

THE SINGER THE SONGS & THE SONG-WRITER

You have a reputation as a songwriter which is as large as the reputation of, say, Burt Bacharach, and probably Cole Porter, and also one as a performer in the tradition of Elvis Presley and the Stones. Everybody who approaches your music approaches it from their perspective. Do you value any aspect of it greater? Do you like to think of yourself, for example, as "Yes, I can write good songs"?

I like to think that, definitely. But I fancy myself as a few things, not in a big-headed way or anything. I really dig myself as a bass player, now more than I have done in the last year, just because we just did a couple of good sessions where I played well.

So as a bass player I kind of fancy myself. As a singer I do, you know, and as a songwriter. Probably comes in that order. But then I can kind of play a bit of keyboards. It just depends on how I'm doing, really, I can play lousy keyboard, too.

With Denny and the others there must be the eternal problem of ego. That is, people are always going to refer to the group as "that's the band with Paul McCartney." How does that weigh on you and how do you think it weighs on them?

If it could happen I'd just like to call it Wings and everyone know that that's the band with Paul McCartney in it, but I don't think it could. So basically, we just call it Paul McCartney and Wings or Paul and Wings to get it as short and as easy to remember as possible. But I think Paul McCartney and Wings will do and whoever joins is just stuck with that. It's a slight hangup but it shouldn't really be a big one. Anyone who's interested in music shouldn't be too hung up by the fact that I'm the front man.

I mean it's Jagger and the Stones in a way, isn't it? He's very definitely the front man and the others all kind of come second, except maybe Keith. But even Keith comes second to Mick, you know. So they haven't done too badly with the ego hangups, have they?

I remember seeing a poster for the Stones years ago with this great big Jagger face. The rest of them were tiny little people. Now I would like to see them all equal and that's the way I feel about them, but obviously for merchandising, marketing and the rest of it, they feel mass appeal is in Jagger's face. And that's what we come down to eventually. Since most people know me better than they're gonna know anybody else in the band, it's silly of us to try to hide it. It's just better to take full advantage of it and just not sweat.

You told me you still ask your friends, "Is this really good?" And Linda mentioned that you still get nervous about the work. And so does this mean you watch critical notices very closely?

No, I don't like criticism whatever. I don't think I ever liked it when my Dad said, I don't like your trousers. But I went through a difficult period where I started to listen to what the newspapers have to say . . . about me . . . and say, some guy would be sittin' in New York all hungup thinking "Well, that's not as good as I woulda wanted." And I thought, "Well, blimey, that's only one guy. I'm not going to take it as gospel."

Linda mentioned you "bounce off" other people. After you left George Martin and the other three, was Linda the only person to bounce your ideas off of?

For a while, yes. Oh yes.

Did you miss not having more people? Is there anyone you ask now outside the band?

Sometimes now I mainly bounce off myself. I do that more now, call it what you will – maturity? Sometimes if a friend is in the studio I'll ask for their opinion and that will make it easier on me. The laugh of all this is I say all this rubbish and it all changes the next day.

I still read the notices and stuff and they're usually bum ones when you're expecting them to be great. Like after *Ram*, there were a lot of bum notices after *Ram*. But I keep meeting people wherever I go, like I met someone skiing. As he skiied past me he said, "I loved *Ram*, Paul." So that's really what I go by, just the kind of people who flash by me in life. Just ordinary people and they said they loved it. That's why I go a lot by sales, not just for the commercial thing. Like if a thing sells well, it means a lot of people bought it and liked it.

Does this mean, then, that you didn't think too much in retrospect of Wild Life. *Because of all your albums. . .*

No, ah, I quite liked it. I must say you have to like me to like the record. I mean, if it's just taken cold, I think it wasn't that brilliant as a recording. We did it in about two weeks, the whole thing. And it had been done on that kind of a buzz we'd been hearing about how Dylan had come in and done everything in one take. I think in fact often we never gave the engineer a chance to even set up a balance. There's a couple of real big songs on there, that freaks or connoisseurs know.

Well, 'Tomorrow.'

Yeah, 'Tomorrow' is one of them. It's like, when I'm talking to people about Picasso or something and they say, well, his blue period was

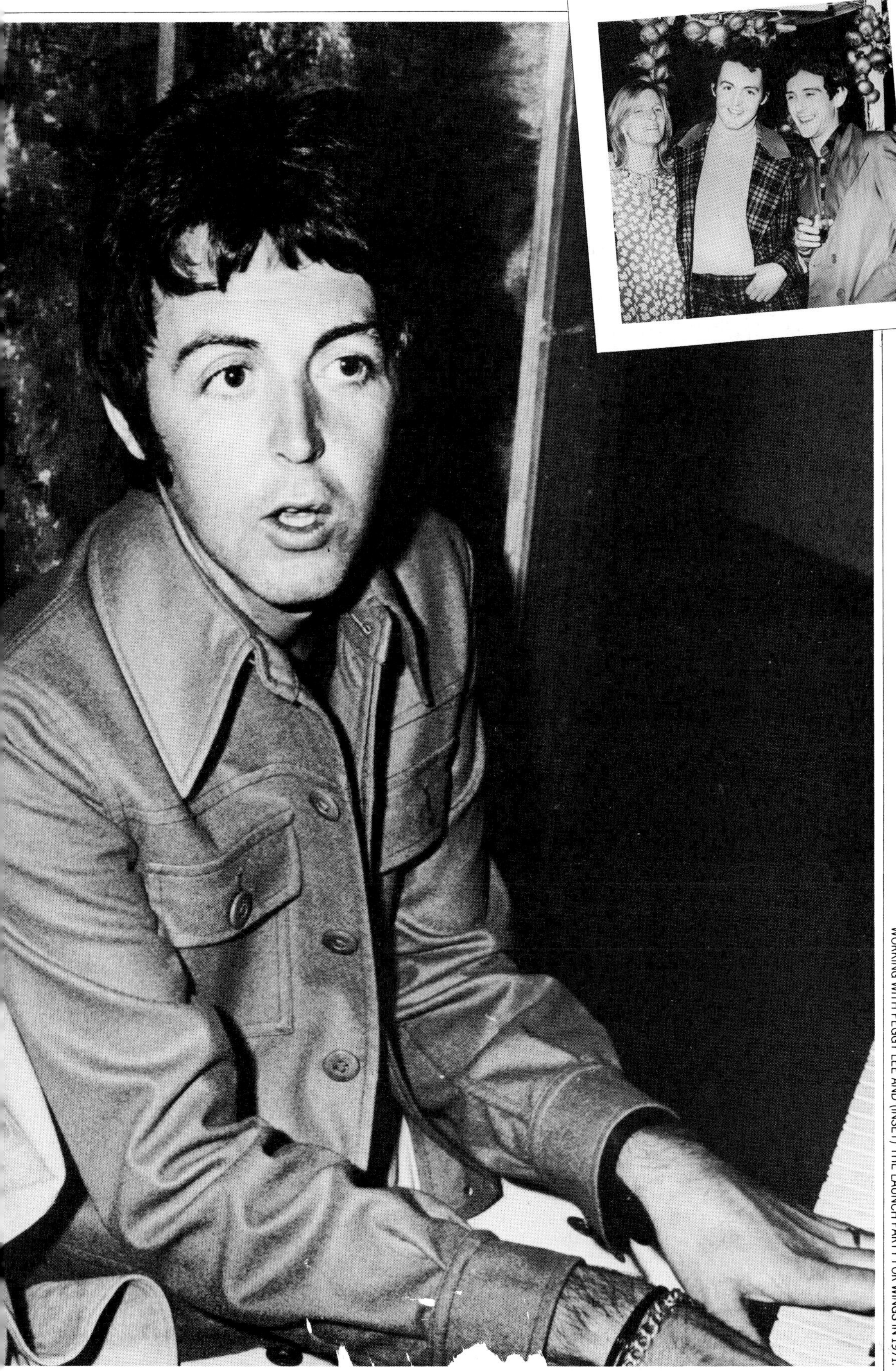

WORKING WITH PEGGY LEE AND (INSET) THE LAUNCH PARTY FOR WINGS IN 1971.

AT THE ABBEY ROAD STUDIOS WITH PRODUCER GEORGE MARTIN.

his only one that was any good. But for me, if the guy does some great things then even his downer moments are interesting. His lesser moments, rather, because they make up the final picture. Some moments seem less, he was going through kind of a pressure period. You know, you can't live your life without pressure periods. No one I know has.

You mentioned Dylan sort of being an inspiration for doing Wild Life *the way you did it... He's going on the road, of course, this month.*

With the Band...

Does this in any way motivate you, inspire you?

No, not particularly. I mean, I've just been on the road last year, so my being ... doing that just might have inspired him. I don't know, you know. He's a great guy, Dylan; he's a musician, and stuff, and he's a great spirit. Love him, you know.

Do you think he influenced you at all?

Oh, yes. Very heavily.

I think the first time was in 'You've Got to Hide Your Love Away.' That was John's song. Then there was a good deal of influence in the 'Hard Day's Night' and 'Help'! periods. Certain chords, the acoustic bit. We liked him.

We met him when he came to New York and we were together awhile. He came to one of my sessions when I was doing *Ram* in New York.

You mentioned in the studio that you were influenced in a recent session by Marvin Gaye's Trouble Man. *Do you think someone might misconstrue this?*

Being influenced by something and stealing something are two different things. When you

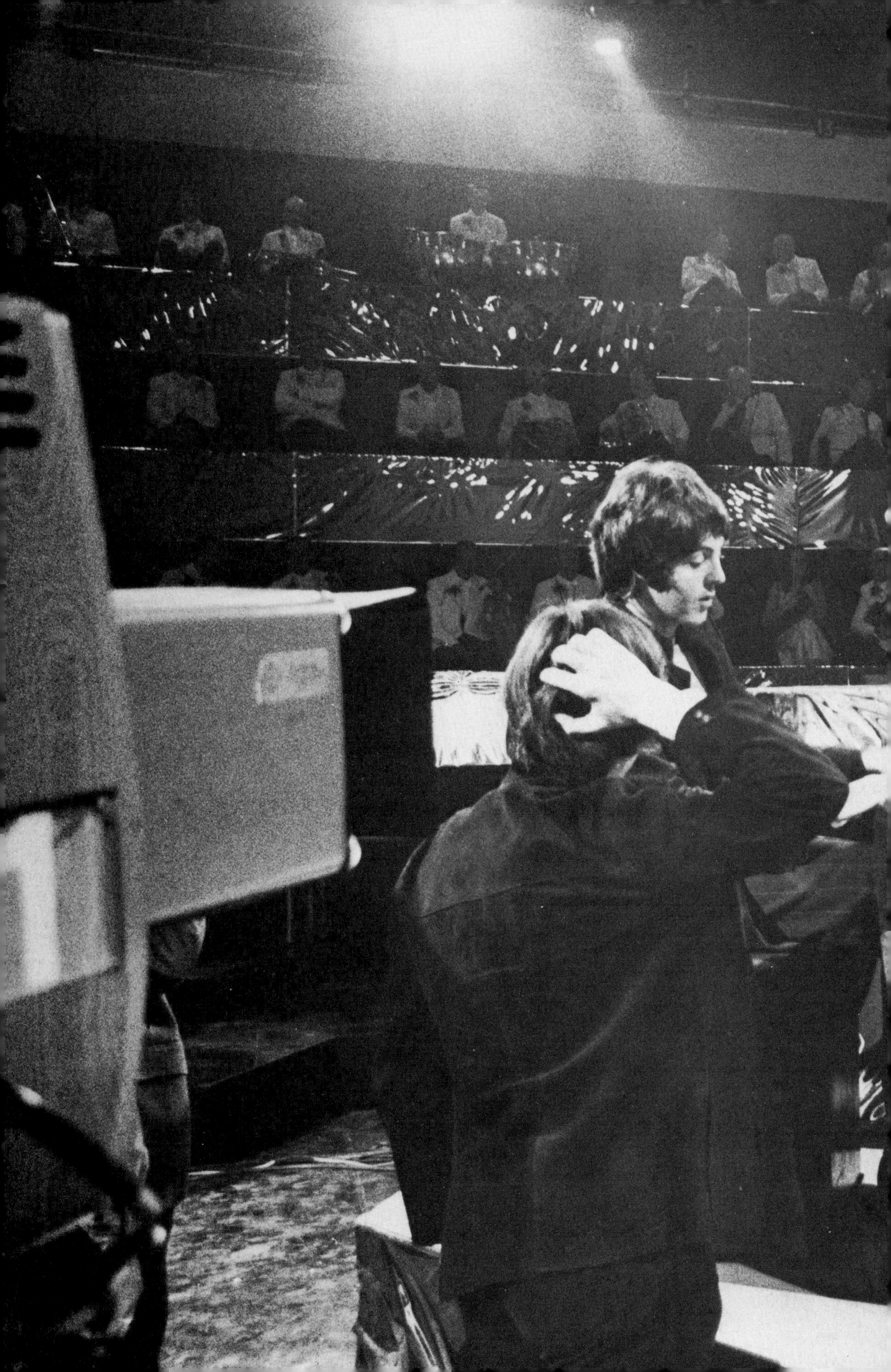

RECORDING 'HEY JUDE' ON THE DAVID FROST SHOW, 1968.

hear the track we did and hear Marvin Gaye's you probably would never know they were related. I may be influenced by something, but it's in my head and doesn't necessarily show in the song. 'Here, There and Everywhere' was supposed to be a Beach Boys song, but you wouldn't have known.

Was it the 'Trouble Man' instrumental?

Yeah. Beautiful, you know. That kind of stuff, I really love. I'd have liked to hear him sing a bit more on it, but it's just good music. It's just good.

We just went to Paris, did one track trying that wasn't too good, and the next track we didn't give a bugger about and it turned out really nice. We played about eleven minutes just jamming, and it all seemed to fit into place.

I've only relearned that in the last four days. Guitar playing is better if you really don't try and if you play like you're playing in the bathroom, playing on the bog, just for yourself. Those are all the great licks, that's when it really happens, you know it's just beautiful then and people can feel that you don't care and it's loose and it's lovely. That's what great musicians have, this kind of feeling that they're not even trying. They just pick up the thing and this great graceful music happens. Basically the thought is to kind of unthink the trying bit. I make better records when I'm just playing for me.

In the songwriting area, you've had thousands of cover versions. There were cover versions in Britain like 'Michelle' by the Overlanders and David and Jonathan, and in America it's ranged from Tony Bennett doing 'My Love' to Vanilla Fudge covering 'Eleanor Rigby.' Ray Charles did a couple. Did you have any feelings about them or didn't you bother to keep track?

Most of them you don't keep track. I don't keep track, but a couple rise to the top. Like Ray Charles' 'Eleanor Rigby' and Roy Redmond's 'Good Day Sunshine.' Great version of that by Roy Redmond.

I'm pleased to see people covering 'My Love' purely out of a business interest, just because it's the first time I've ever come near to owning one of my copyrights. Strange, but it *is* true, you know. So I've got a renewed interest if someone does it.

But the actual versions I normally don't really like. For some reason I think people don't seem to get behind the songs for my taste, except, say, Ray Charles, some of the really good people, will get behind one. I haven't heard Tony Bennett's 'My Love.'

Was 'My Love' written for Linda?

Yes.

Was Mother Mary ('Let It Be') a reference to the Virgin Mary?

No. My mother's name was Mary. So that was probably what that was about.

Are any of your characters inspired by real people – 'Michelle', 'Uncle Albert', 'Eleanor Rigby'.

'Uncle Albert' was. I did have an uncle Albert who used to quote the Bible to everyone when

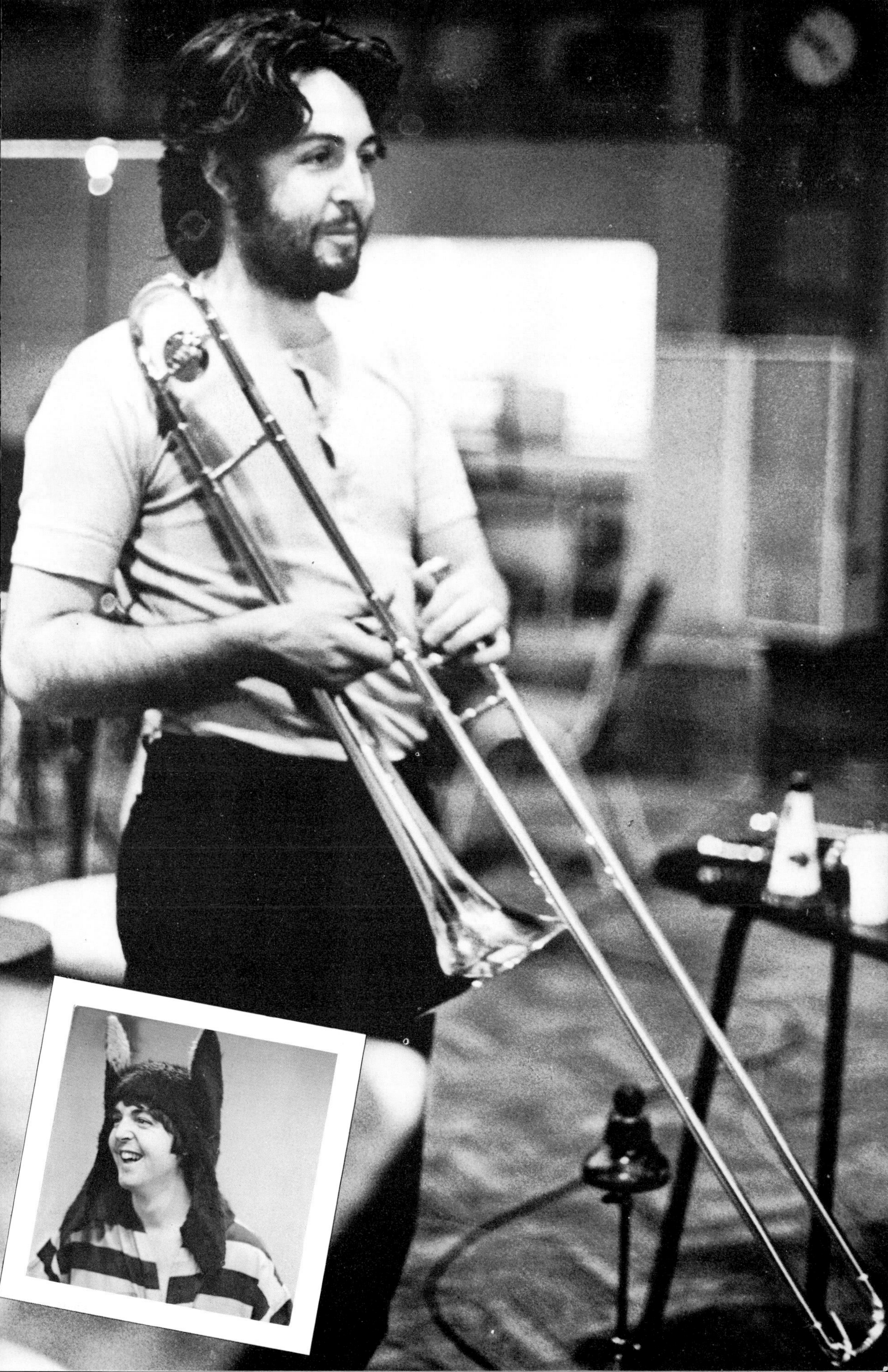

he got drunk. He used to read from the Bible. It was the only time he ever read the Bible, but it was when he was drunk. He died a few years ago and he was a good man. So he was kind of inspirational. 'Michelle' is just a name. 'Eleanor Rigby', that was just a name. That was just made up.

There is actual French in the song 'Michelle' and on 'Drink to Me.'

Yes, there is French on 'Michelle.' On 'Drink to Me' it's just a background kind of thing.

What made you think of doing the French in 'Michelle'?

I just fancied writing some French words and I had a friend whose wife taught French and we were kind of sitting around and I just asked her, you know, what we could figure out that was French. We got words that go together well. It was mainly because I always used to think the song always sounded like a French thing (imitates French singing, Charles Aznavour style). And I can't speak French, really, so we sorted out some actual words.

The big copyright off the McCartney *album was 'Maybe I'm Amazed.' Were you aware that would go down so well?*

Sometimes we're a bit daft here. We have a bit of funky organization, you know, which isn't that clued in to picking up tracks off albums. At the time we thought 'Maybe I'm Amazed' was a good track and maybe we should do that as a single, which it probably should have been. But we never did. It was the same with 'Uncle Albert' in Britain. We only did that as a single in America and it was a great success there. It would have been a big success here, I think, but for some silly little reason it never managed to get out.

Yeah, I'd say 'Maybe I'm Amazed' was the most successful song off *McCartney.* You've got people who say "Oh, I love The Lovely Linda" and silly things that were just little asides on the album.

Or 'That Would Be Something.' They were almost throwaways, you know. But that's why they were included – they weren't quite throwaways. That was the whole idea of the album. All the normal things that you record that are great and have all this atmosphere but aren't that brilliant as recordings or production jobs. Normally that stuff ends up with the rest of your demos, but all that stuff is often stuff I love. I've got a tape of 'Fixing a Hole' which is somewhere in my house under a big lump of tapes. It's great because on the tape I'm writing 'Fixing a Hole,' and I'm going through all these words and it goes on for hours, gradually getting the tune.

'Give Ireland Back to the Irish' was the first of your singles in eight years that didn't sell in America and Britain.

Before I did that, I always used to think, God, John's crackers, doing all these political songs. I understand he really feels deeply, you know. So do I. I hate all that Nixon bit, all that Ireland bit, and oppression anywhere. I think our mob do, our generation do hate that and wish it could be changed, but up until the actual time when the

ON THE SET OF 'HELP'.

paratroopers went in and killed a few people, a bit like Kent State, the moment when it is actually there on the doorstep, I always used to think it's still cool to not say anything about it, because it's not going to sell anyway and no one's gonna be interested.

So I tried it, it was Number One in Ireland and, funnily enough, it was Number One in Spain, of all places. I don't think Franco could have understood.

Then the second, and to date the only other one that didn't make it that big, was 'Mary Had a Little Lamb.' Do you think that was the start of the "So it's come to this" type of attitude?

Yeah, I should think so. Probably. Yeah. You see, I do things that aren't necessarily very carefully thought out. Now, you know, I've just got three kids over the last few years, and when I am sitting at home playing at the piano my audience a lot of the time is the kids. I just wrote that one up, the words were already written, you know, I just found out what the words to the nursery rhyme were, wrote a little tune up around it, went and recorded it. I had an idea in my head that it would be interesting for everyone to find out what the words to the original nursery rhyme were. I thought it was all very deep and all very nice. I see now, you know, it wasn't much of a record. That's all. It just didn't really make it as a record, and that's what tells, the black plastic.

'Hi Hi Hi' was the one that brought you back to the top ten, after 'Give Ireland Back to the Irish' and 'Mary Had a Little Lamb,' although in Britain they played 'C Moon' because 'Hi Hi Hi' was banned by the BBC.

I thought the 'Hi Hi Hi' thing could easily be taken as a natural high, could be taken as booze high and everything. It doesn't have to be drugs, you know, so I'd kind of get away with it. Well, the first thing they saw was drugs, so I didn't get away with that, and then I just had some line 'Lie on the bed and get ready for my polygon.'

The daft thing about all of that was our publishing company, Northern Songs, owned by Lew Grade, got the lyrics wrong and sent them round to the radio station and it said, 'Get ready for my body gun,' which is far more suggestive than anything I put. 'Get ready for my polygon,' watch out baby, I mean it was suggestive, but abstract suggestive, which I thought I'd get away with. Bloody company goes round and makes it much more specific by putting "body gun." Better words, almost.

It made it anyway in the States.

Yeah, well, the great laugh is when we go live, it makes a great announcement. You can say "This one was banned!" and everyone goes "Hooray!" The audience love it, you know. "This next one was banned!" and then you get raving, because everyone likes to. Everyone's a bit anti-all-that-banning, all that censorship. Our crew, our generation, really doesn't dig that stuff, as I'm sure you know.

George Martin gave me the impression you'd written the basic tune to 'Live and Let Die' and said to him, as one might say to a drummer, I'd like X seconds of this type of music. Is that what you did?

Nah. I sort of wrote it, got George round to my house, sat down at the piano, worked out an arrangement with him, then he went off and scored it. Because I can't do that, I can't voice instruments and stuff. I can in my head, but I don't know how to get it all down. I'll say, tell the cellos to play A, and he'll say, "Oh, of course, in their range that's a B flat," or something like that. I can just give him the piano things. So we worked it up and then we went into the studio and did it in just a couple of days. It was quite easy to do and turned out well for the film.

It was certainly your biggest production job of the last five years.

Definitely.

Because of George?

Because of Bond. I didn't feel that I could go and do a little acoustic number for a Bond film. What are people going to think, "Oh, Christ, what is this?"

With the shadow of Shirley Bassey in their minds.

Exactly. You're following something so you've got to keep vaguely within the format.

'Helen Wheels' has done better in America than England, as have many of your records past, back to the old days. Have you ever thought of a reason why?

The only thing I can think of is the foreigner syndrome. We're British, and that means something to an American. It's like some Americans who do better over here, like Cassidy and the Osmonds, even Elvis.

When you started to play live again in 1972 with Wings, *were you very nervous?*

Yes. Very nervous. The main thing I didn't want to face was the torment of five rows of press people with little pads all looking and saying, "Oh well, he's not as good as he was." So we decided to go out on that university tour, which made me less nervous because it was less of a big deal. We went out on that tour and by the end of that I felt quite ready for something else, and we went to Europe. I was pretty scared on the European tour. That was a bit more of the big deal, here he is, ladies and gentlemen, sold all the tickets out... I had to go on with a band I really didn't know much. We decided not to do any Beatle material, which was a killer, of course, because it meant we had to do an hour of other material, and we didn't have it, then. I didn't have something like 'My Love' that was sort of mine. I felt like everyone wanted Beatles stuff, so I was pretty nervous on that.

But by the end of the European tour I felt better, and at the end of the British tour I felt good. By the time we did the British tour I knew we could get it easily and that I could get it going. Everyone digs it, and there's enough stuff not to be nervous.

WINGS IN FLIGHT: BAND ON THE RUN.

Is Band on the Run *a concept that refers to the band?*

Our band? I've been thinking about that since you asked me yesterday. I don't really know, to tell you the truth. It's just a good flow of words. I really don't analyze stuff, and if I do I kind of remember what it meant about three months later, just lying in bed one night.

It started off with 'If I ever get out of here.' That came from a remark George made at one of the Apple meetings. He was saying that we were all prisoners in some way, some kind of remark like that. "If we ever get out of here," the prison bit, and I thought that would be a nice way to start an album. A million reasons, really. I can never lay them all down. It's a million things, I don't like to analyze them, all put together. *Band on the Run* – escaping, freedom, criminals. You name it, it's there.

Some of the people on the cover, like (BBC talk show host and author) Michael Parkinson, aren't known in America. How did you design that?

We were just lying in bed at night, as is our wont, thinking what shall we do for the album cover.

As is –

As again is our wont, every year, every album you go through it. We thought *Band on the Run,* let's have a group of people caught in a spotlight as if they're trying to escape from jail. We thought, well, we'll use actors, and then we thought, no, that's not really going to mean much, so we thought, let's try and get different people who are personalities from various walks of life.

So it's just a group of personalities who all look like they're prisoners escaping, but when you look a little closer you find James Coburn's in there and John Conteh, who's a British boxer from Liverpool. Just various people, just for the lark.

People you liked?

Sort of. They're not necessarily our favourite people in the world.

I didn't mean this was another Sergeant Pepper *cover. . .*

No, no, it's not that kind of thing at all. It's not cult idols, it hasn't anything to do with that. It's just a group of people, and if you're going to have a group of people, why not make them interesting? So we rang all the people up and Coburn said "Sure, man, be real pleased to do it." He was great.

Were you planning originally to play any drums?

Not at all. Our drummer rang up an hour before we left for Lagos to record and said "I can't make this Africa trip," so we said "Oh, I see, thank you very much, cheerio." We just trucked off to Lagos and I thought, "Christ, what are we going to do now? Well, I fancy playing drums anyway, I like playing drums," and Stevie (Wonder) had just done a couple of albums playing drums, so I thought I'd do it.

Am I correct in assuming he's your biggest idol, as it were?

He's one of them. I think he's great, I really do.

Did you ever get any feedback on the album cover of Red Rose Speedway, *the message to him ("We love you" to Stevie in braille)?*

Just that he knew about it and he dug it. You know, nods and winks.

So our drummer [Denny Seiwell] didn't want to come to Africa. I don't know quite why. We're all going to Africa to record and if the drummer won't come, what do you do? You don't say "Well, we'll see you when we get back, thanks a lot, we understand." You say "Well, er, ummmmm," and he leaves.

I think (guitarist) Henry McCulloch came to a head one day when I was asking him to play something he didn't really fancy playing. We all got a bit choked about it, and he rang up later and said he was leaving. I said, "Well, OK." That's how that happened. You know, with the kind of music we play, a guitarist has got to be a bit adaptable. It was just one of those things. I don't think there was anything wrong with them as musicians, they were both good musicians, but they just didn't fit in.

Then there was trouble in Nigeria with Fela Ransome Kuti (ex-Ginger Baker's Air Force).

You heard about that? All it was was we were recording in Lagos. Lately we've gone to two different places to record, just for the fun of it. We've been to Lagos and to Paris and in both of the places they say, "Why did you come here? You've got much better studios in England or America, you must be daft!" And we say, "Well, it's just for the fun, it's just to come somewhere different for a different type of turn-on, that's all." They never really seem to be able to understand it. I think old Fela, when he found us in Lagos, thought, "Hello, why have they come to Lagos?" And the only reason he could think of was that we must be stealing black music, black African music, the Lagos sound, we'd come down there to pick it up. So I said, "Do us a favour, we do OK as it is, we're not pinching your music."

They felt that they have their own little ethnic thing going and these big foreigners are

ON STAGE WITH WINGS GUITARIST HENRY McCULLOUGH.

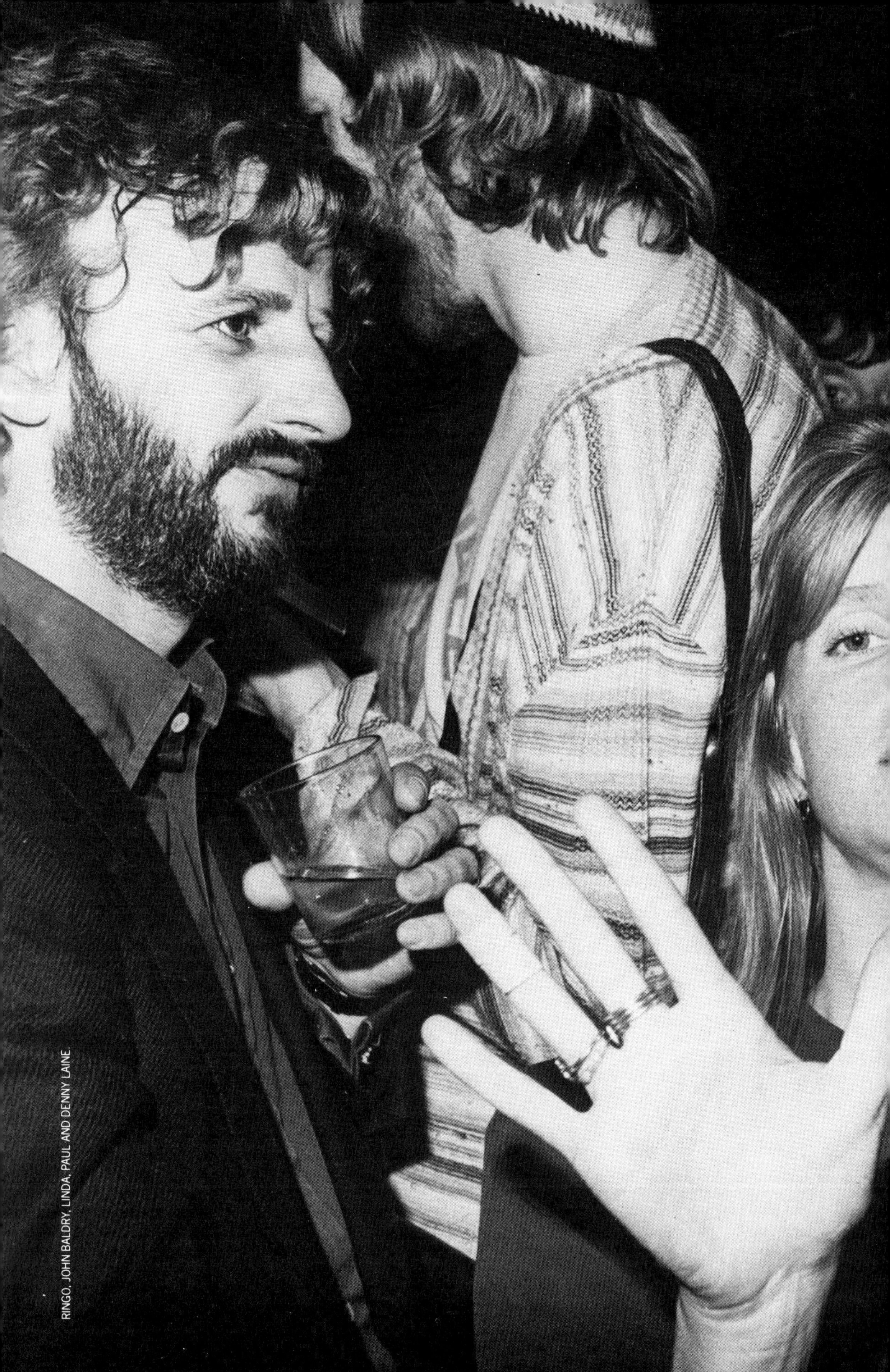

RINGO, JOHN BALDRY, LINDA, PAUL AND DENNY LAINE.

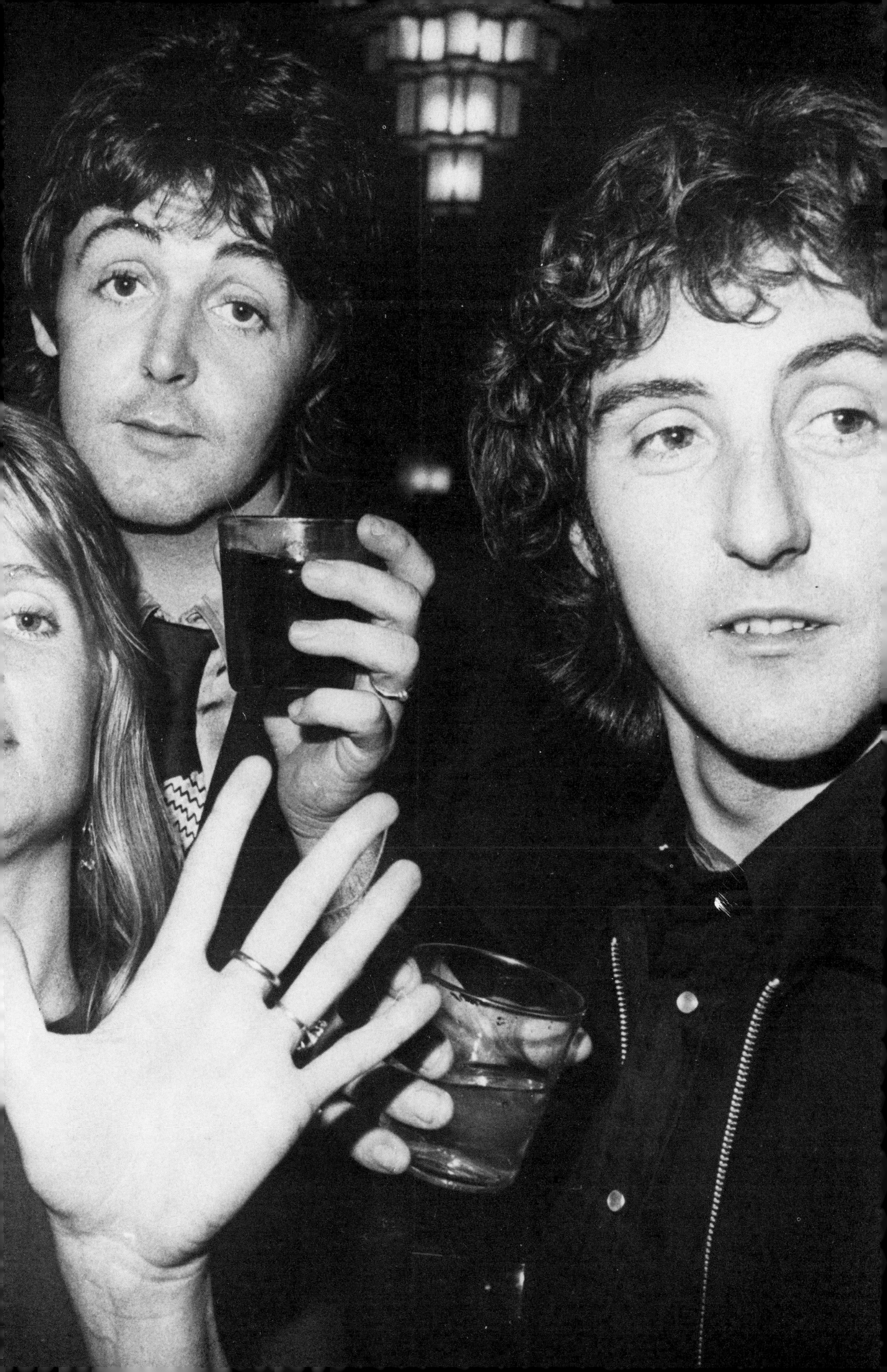

WITH PLATINUM DISC FOR BAND ON THE RUN IN LOS ANGELES.

taking all their bit and beating them back to the West with it. Because they have a lot of difficulty getting their sound heard in the West. There's not an awful lot of demand, except for things like, what was it, "Soul Makossa." Except for that kind of thing they don't really get heard.

And they are brilliant, it's incredible music down there. I think it will come to the fore. And I thought my visit would, if anything, help them, because it would draw attention to Lagos and people would say, "Oh, by the way, what's the music down there like?" and I'd say it was unbelievable. It is unbelievable. When I heard Fela Ransome-Kuti the first time, it made me cry, it was that good.

Can you tell the story about Dustin Hoffman and 'Drink to Me?'

Sure. We were in Jamaica on holiday and we were staying in a little house outside Montego Bay, and we read in the local newspaper, *The Daily Gleaner*, that Dustin Hoffman and Steve McQueen were in town filming *Papillon*. They were just along the coast from us. We were saying it would be great to meet him, have dinner with him, so Linda rang up. She's good at that, I'm always a bit embarrassed. So Linda talked to his wife and suggested having us for dinner. So they said, great, love to see you, they were a bit bored, they weren't too keen on Jamaica, so we went around to their house one night.

We got friendly and were chatting away. We'd been talking about songwriting, and Dustin was saying he thought it was an incredible gift to be able to write a song about something. People think that, but I always maintain it's the same as any gift. It probably is more magical because it's music, and I think it is more magical. But take his acting talent. It's great. I was saying it's the same as you and acting, when the man says "Action!" you just pull it out of the bag, don't you? You don't know where it comes from, you just do it! How do you get all of your characterizations? It's just in you. The same with me. With a song, I just pull it out of the air. I knock a couple of chords off, and it suggests a melody to me. If I haven't heard the melody before, I'll keep it.

So he says, you mean you can just do it, like that? He was lovely, Dustin. (Does Dustin Hoffman impersonation.) "You can just do it?" I was saying, I think so. We went back a couple of days later and he said, "I've been thinking about this I've seen a little in *Time* magazine about Picasso, and it struck me as being very poetic. I think this would be really great set to music." It was just a little piece out of *Time*. It was one of those Passed On bits, you know, Transition or whatever they call it. (Sees unusually dressed studio assistant.) Transvestite... So he says, there's a little story here. In the article he supposedly said "Drink to me, drink to my health, you know I can't drink any more." He went to paint a bit, and then he went to bed at three in the morning. He didn't wake up the next morning and they found him, dead. Dustin thought "Drink to me, drink to my health, you know I can't drink anymore" was a great parting remark. They were Picasso's last words. So he said "Could you write something to that?"

I happened to have my guitar with me, I'd brought it around, and I said, yeah, sure. I strummed a couple of chords I knew I couldn't go wrong on and started singing 'Drink to me, drink to my health,' and he leaps out of his chair and says "Annie! Annie!" That's his wife. He says, "Annie! Annie!" The most incredible thing! He's doing it! He's writing it! It's coming out!" He's leaping up and down, just like in the films, you know. And I'm knocked out because he's so appreciative. I was writing the tune there and he was well chuffed.

Then we went to Nigeria and we were working in Ginger's studio, Ginger Baker/ARC Studio in Lagos, nice studio down there. We thought we'd do this Picasso number, and we started off doing it straight. Then we thought, Picasso was kind of far out in his pictures, he'd done all these different kinds of things, fragmented, cubism, and the whole bit. I thought it would be nice to get a track a bit like that, put it through different moods, cut it up, edit it, mess around with it – like he used to do with his pictures. You see the old films of him painting, he paints it once and if he doesn't like it he paints it again, right on top of it, and by about twenty-five times he's got his picture. So we tried to use this kind of idea, I don't know much about it, to tell you the truth, but what we did know we tried to get in the song, sort of a Cubist thing.

So Ginger, he helped on a few little things of it. At the end, where we go "Ho, hey, ho." We did the cutting up there. Then we got Ginger and a couple of people from around the studio and we got little tin cans and filled them with gravel from outside the studio, and used them as shakers, so at the end you hear this (makes shaking gravel noise), and that's Ginger and a big mob of us going (gravel noise again). So we just made it all up and then edited the tape. There were about four or five big edits in it, really.

'Jet' comes back in.

'Jet' comes back in, right.

Any reason for that?

Just the idea of his different periods, this comes back in, it's all a big muddle. We were just making it up as we went along. We didn't have any big concept of it in mind at all. I just thought, we'll mess it up, keep messing it up until it sounds good, like Picasso did, with the instinctive knowledge you've got. So that's how that one came about.

You mentioned Ginger. I just read a rumour a few days ago about Cream reforming. The rumour happens to be false. But why do you think so many people want the big groups to reform?

A lot of people do. I think if you've got a band together that works, I don't think people ever see why you break it up. In the case of those three, if they're not doing much in other people's minds, there's no reason why they shouldn't be

back together, as far as those people are concerned. It's always a nice idea.

You've said 'Jet' is a puppy. Whose puppy?

We've got a Labrador puppy who is a runt, the runt of a litter. We bought her along a roadside in a little pet shop, out in the country one day. She was a bit of a wild dog, a wild girl who wouldn't stay in. We have a big wall around our house in London, and she wouldn't stay in, she always used to jump the wall. She'd go out on the town for the evening, like 'Lady and the Tramp'. She must have met up with some big black Labrador or something. She came back one day pregnant. She proceeded to walk into the garage and have this litter. How many, nine?

Linda: Seven.

Seven. Seven little black puppies, perfect little black Labradors, and she's not black, she's tan. So we worked out it must have been a black Labrador. What we do is if either of the dogs we have has a litter, we try to keep them for the puppy stage, so we get the best bit of them, and then when they get a bit unmanageable we ask people if they want to have a puppy. So 'Jet' was one of the puppies. We give them all names. We've had some great names, there was one puppy called Golden Molasses. I rather like that. Then there was one called Brown Megs, named after a Capitol executive (Laughs.) They've all gone now. The people change the names if they don't like them.

The "suffragette" business has nothing to do with Jet.

No. I make up so much stuff. It means something to me when I do it, and it means something to the record buyer, but if I'm asked to analyze it I can't really explain what it is. 'Suffragette' was crazy enough to work. It sounded silly, so I liked it.

Where were the orchestra bits on the album done?

In London. They were done with Tony Visconti. He does a lot of people. He's married to Mary Hopkin . . . or Mary Hopkin is married to him. He was nice, he came around to the house one day and we worked out the arrangements. We just did it one day at Air London Studios, all the overdubs.

The noises at the end of 'Mrs. Vanderbilt' –

The laughing? It started off in Africa. We were doing sort of daft laughs at the end. When we got back we eventually overdubbed this crowd of people who were laughing. It was great listening to the tapes, trying to select the little bit of laughter that we would use. Most of it was us, but we need a little bit to cushion it up. It was great listening to a roomful of people laughing in stereo. They were getting into all these laughing bits, and we were on the floor.

Is Helen Wheels your land rover?

Helen Wheels is our land rover. It's a name we gave to our land rover, which is a trusty vehicle that gets us around Scotland. It takes us up to the Shetland Islands and down to London. The song starts off in Glasgow, then it goes past Carlisle, goes to Kendal, Liverpool, Birmingham

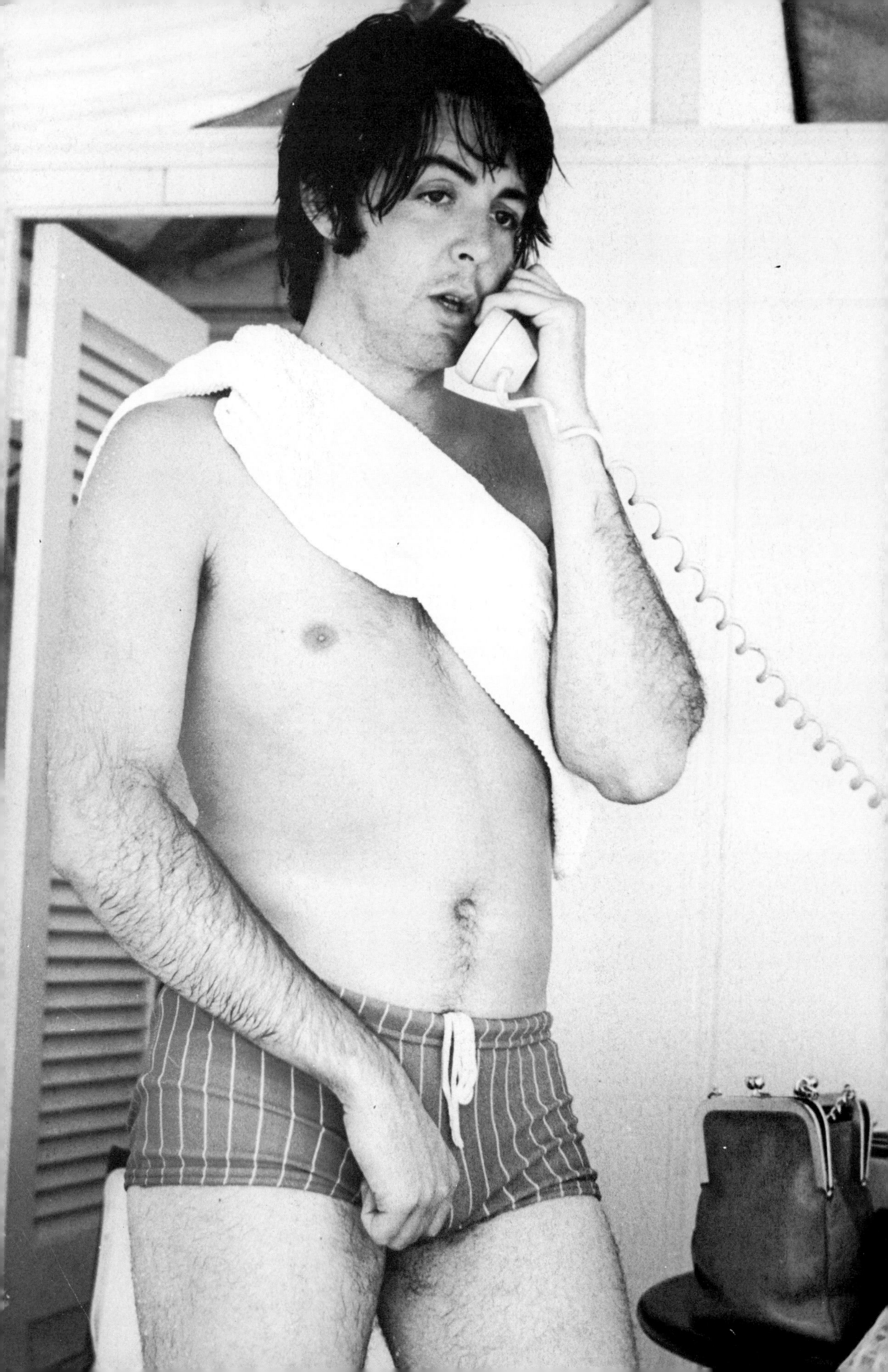

THE McCARTNEY FAMILY ON WINGS TOUR IN BERLIN.

WITH BROTHER MIKE McGEAR AND (INSET) THE BUST IN GOTENBURG, SWEDEN 1972.

and London. It's the route coming down from our Scottish farm to London, so it's really the story of a trip down. Little images along the way.

Do they "play the West Coast sound" in Liverpool?

Liverpool's on the West Coast of England, so that's all that means.

Is merchandising why 'Helen Wheels' is on the American Band on the Run *and not the British?*

Yes. We got a call from one of the Capitol executives saying "Paul, you know we took 'Money' off the Pink Floyd album *(Dark Side of the Moon)* and after it became a hit single the album did so many extra units. What do you say we put 'Helen Wheels' and we'll do so many extra units. So I phoned him back the next day and told him it sounded OK to me.

Did you choose 'Nineteen Hundred and Eighty-Five' because that's one year after 1984?

No. You see, with a lot of songs I do, the first line is it. It's all in the first line, and then you have to go on and write the second line. With 'Eleanor Rigby' I had "picks up the rice in the church were the wedding has been." that was the one big line that started me off on it. With this one it was "No one ever left alive in nineteen hundred and eighty-five." That's all I had of that song for months. "No one ever left alive in nineteen hundred and eighty... six?" It wouldn't have worked!

You said you didn't intend to make 'Let Me Roll It' sound like John.

I still don't think it sounds like him, but that's your opinion. I can dig it if it sounds that way to you. I listened to that album last night over at Linda's sister's place. We had a little sit-around, a little get-together there.

I love the album, I must say. When you make an album you're waiting for everyone to criticize, waiting for everyone to put it down. You're living on your nerves, really, for the first couple of weeks, wondering if it's going to be the biggest blow-out of all-time, or whether it's going to be as good as you think it is. Having listened to it last night for the first time in a couple of weeks and having forgotten it almost, I must say it's great, I love it. I really got off on it last night.

You've given identity bracelets?

It's for all the people who worked on the album. They haven't got them yet, but they're in the post. It's nice after you've done something that everyone's enjoyed to give them a little souvenir of it. We copped one each for ourselves, too.

Are they credited on the sleeve?

No, they just get bracelets and we say "Thanks to EMI, Lagos." They're not playing on the record. In fact, the only other musician on the album, other than the orchestra, is, funnily enough, African! We were gonna use African musicians, but when we were told we were about to pinch the music we thought "Well, up you, we'll do it ourselves then, so there's no question about it." Then we were back in London working at Air Studios and this old friend from the past named Remi Kabaka turns up. And he's from Lagos! He played on one of the tracks, he plays a bit of percussion on 'Bluebird,' so he's the only one who ended up doing anything on the album.

You're playing what sounds like kazoo on 'You're Sixteen,' Ringo's song.

It's not kazoo. It sounds like a kazoo, but it's me doing an imitation. (Does imitation of a saxophone.) It was put through a fuzz thing. It's a bit daft, really, because it winds up sounding like a kazoo, I could have just done it on a kazoo. The idea was to make it sound like a great big funky sax.

The song is a big hit now.

It's nice, I heard it a lot last night on the radio.

Did you overdub your part on an already-finished vocal?

Yeah, I went down to the session one night when I was doing 'Six O'Clock,' on the same album, at the same time. At the end of the session they were playing it back and they said "We need a solo here."

Which of your songs do you think you'd do if you toured now?

I must say I wouldn't mind doing Beatles songs, but it's just a little bit funny. People might want to hear Beatles stuff out of nostalgia, but you don't want to just live on your laurels. You want to try and create a whole new thing, so you can say, "Well, this is me." *Then*, once you've established yourself, you can do the Beatles stuff. That's the way I felt, really. It's good now, because we've got a good mixture. I could do 'Blackbird,' or 'Let It Be,' or 'Long and Winding Road,' something like that.

Do you ever think of your contributions to music?

I don't analyze it, I think about it.

What do you think your contribution has been?

I don't know, you know. I just figure I can do it, quite well. He said, attempting to be modest! But I think I can do it quite well. If you have a song you want me to write, I can manage it. I'm quite proud of the fact that I can do it. It's like someone who can strip a car down. I'd be just as proud of that. It's just that music is the same for me as any talent, it's no big deal. I'm glad I can do it.

Do you think there is life after youth in rock? Can someone rock in their thirties?

Sure. (Linda starts to dance.) Definitely. The question is really whether you do it when you're in your thirties. What happens is that when you reach your thirties you may feel a little less like doing it. But you might feel more like doing it. I mean, Jagger's leaping around more than he's ever leapt around. So it just depends on yourself. I'm sure there's no big thing about being through in your thirties, the twenties were it. You've got Fred Astaire, he was forty and nipping around like a lad of twelve.

You're happy?

Yes.

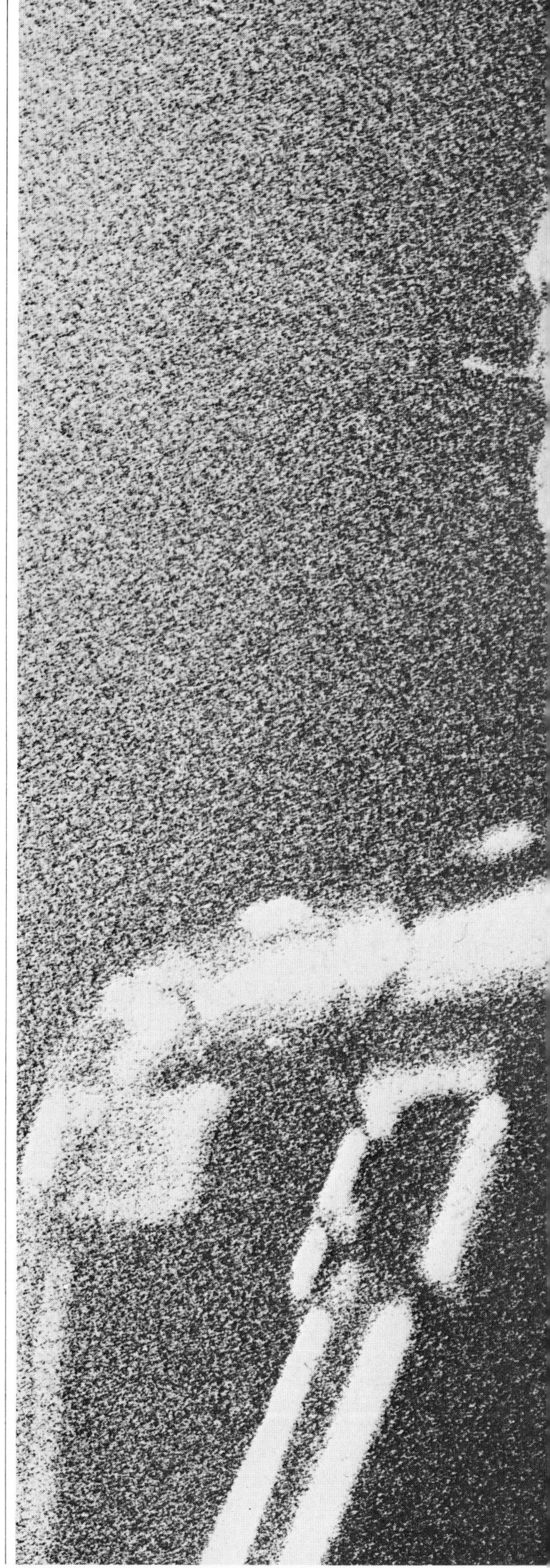

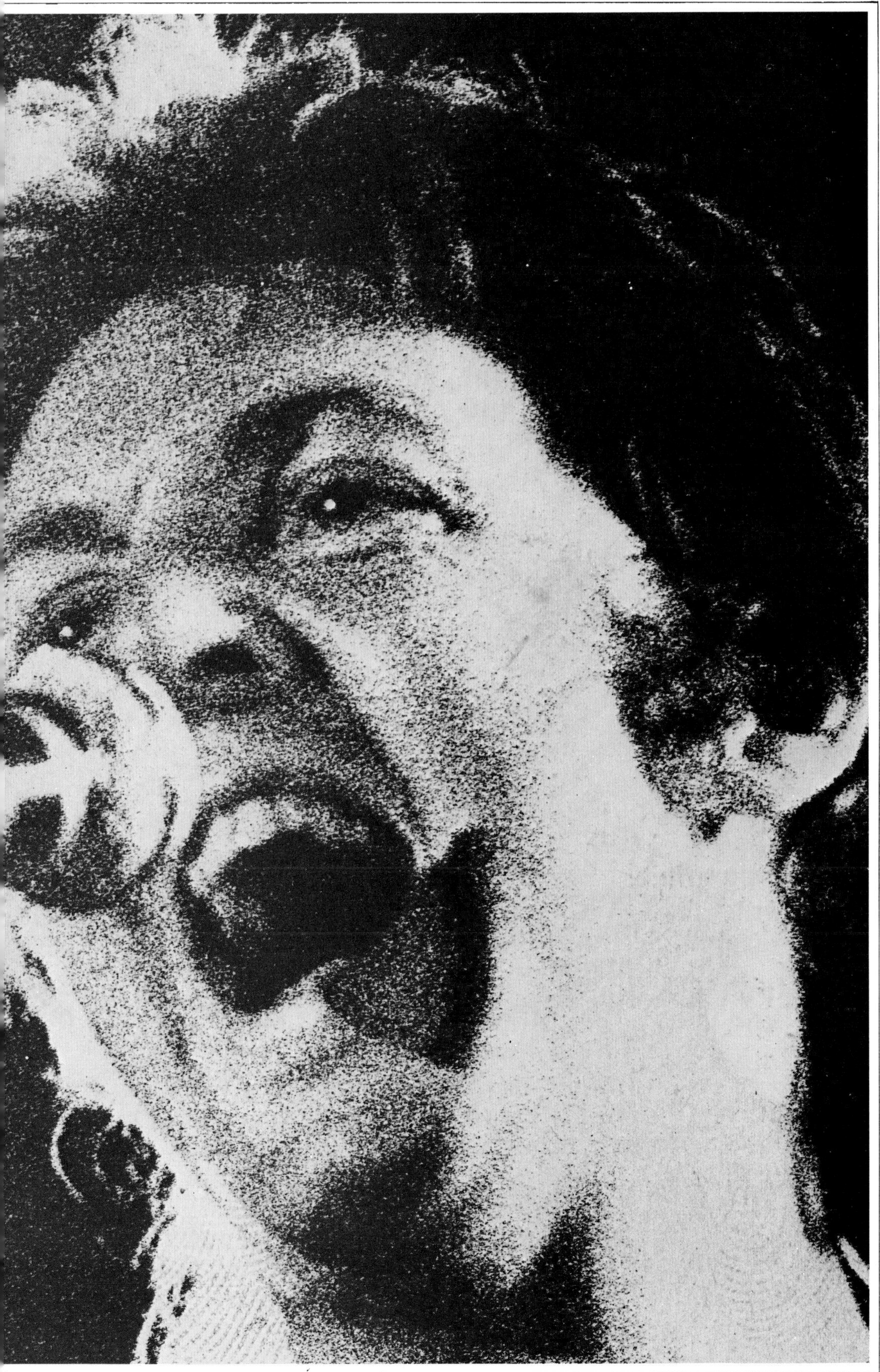

VENUS & MARS ARE ALRIGHT.

It was the first time Paul McCartney had heard his new single played on the radio. 'Listen to What the Man Said' had gone straight on the Capitol Radio playlist, and that Monday afternoon Paul and Linda heard the song as Paul manipulated their Rolls Royce convertible through the narrow streets of London's Mayfair.

"Sounds good," the lead Wing decided. "It's a good summer single." As if to prove it, Capitol Radio went into a medley from *Pet Sounds.*

"There's a funny story about that one," McCartney smiled. "It was one of the songs we'd gone in with high hopes for. Whenever I would play it on the piano, people would say 'Oh, I like that one.' But when we did the backing track, we thought we didn't really get it together at all. We let it stay and added some things on it, Dave Mason came in and we did a little bit of overdubbing guitars, and then we wondered what we could do for a solo. We thought it would be great to have a very technical musician come in and do a great lyrical solo.

"Someone said 'Tom Scott lives near here.' We said, yeah, give him a ring, see if he turns up, and he turned up within half an hour! There he was, with his sax, and he sat down in the studio playing through. The engineer was recording it. We kept all the notes he was playing casually. He came in and I said 'I think that's it.' He said 'Did you record that?' I said yes, and we listened to it back. No one could believe it, so he went out and tried a few more, but they weren't as good. He'd had all the feel on this early take, the first take. So we'd finished the session, we just sat around and chatted for a couple of hours. I think what he plays on that song is lovely and that, overall, it worked."

For Paul McCartney to expound on one of his songs at that length was to be uncharacteristically talkative, but he was riding a wave of good luck uncharacteristic even for him. *Band on the Run* had recently won a Grammy for the Best Vocal Group Performance of 1974, *Venus and Mars* had unearthly advance orders of one and a half million, 'Junior's Farm' had extended America's longest string of consecutive top ten singles to seven, and his lawyers had just completed negotiation of his new contract with EMI and Capitol, a contract with provisions so generous some shareholders protested on the grounds that Capitol did not have the resources to make such an offer.

"I always feel dull doing interviews," McCartney admitted, facing an afternoon of interviews to promote *Venus and Mars.* "I'd like to have great stories to tell. But I don't have a lot of control, or I don't feel I have a lot of control, over some songs."

As the McCartney mobile worked its way toward a Knightsbridge restaurant, one was constantly reminded of the appropriateness of Lee Eastman's admonition to his son-in-law to "make sure you stay ordinary." Paul was constantly recognized at every intersection and photographed by camera – carrying tourists at every red light. "Man, I don't believe who I'm talking to," a travelling Canadian student quaked near Piccadilly. "Can you pose with my wife?" a honeymooning Italian begged. McCartney granted every request: for this sunny lunchtime, he was in an outgoing mood.

This wasn't to say that everything was a source of joy. As he parked his car outside an Italian restaurant Paul addressed the immediate dilemma posed by the Robert Stigwood Organization's desire to film the West End play *John Paul, George, Ringo and Bert.*

"I'm not struck on it. The original thing was

THE NEW WINGS BACKSTAGE.

written for a theatre presentation up in Liverpool at the Everyman (Theatre). A lot of people went up there thinking, hello, it's about the Beatles, could be a lot of money in this. The playwright who wrote it is a little Liverpool bloke and he's written a nice play but in the play it's almost not important what the story is. He's sort of taken all the press handouts that there ever were about the Beatles without really going into the history. He's just made a pastiche of it.

"It's very funny, and I've read the script. A lot of people like it. But now they want to make a film, and to me it seems that a film is going to be like The Beatles Life Story, inevitably. The plot of this little play is so weird and so wrong. Linda appears in a kind of crazy light. So do I. I appear as this total business-like character, which I only was towards the end of the thing. George is made to be a religious freak. It has nothing to do with how the Beatles were. My basic objection is that if they're going to do a thing which in years to come is going to look like the official Beatles story, they must at least think about getting it right.

Also, they're not thinking of bothering to give us a percentage, and I think that as it's our life and we're still living, that's a bit rich,"

Venus and Mars employed a few of the techniques McCartney learned while a Beatle. He pointed out that the album had more links than anything he had worked on since *Abbey Road.* An example was the segue between 'Listen to What the Man Said' and 'Treat Her Gently/Lonely Old People,' the latter track in itself a medley. The bridge was retained on the 'Listen to What the Man Said' single. "You either have to leave it and stop 'Listen to What the Man Said' dead or you spill over into the next little link piece. I just like that link myself, and thought no one's going to mind that little extra on the record."

Paul's penchant for "top and tail" ing an album, manifested in *Sgt. Pepper's Lonely Hearts Club Band* and *Band on the Run,* was further exhibited in the appearance on the new album of two variations of *Venus and Mars.* Popular speculation had the McCartneys as the little couple.

"When we had a party in the States to celebrate having finished the album, someone came up to us and said 'Hello, Venus. Hello, Mars.' I thought, 'Oh, no." When I write songs, I'm not necessarily talking about me, although psychoanalysts would say "Yes, you are, mate." But as far as I'm concerned, I'm not.

"The song 'Venus and Mars' is about an imaginary friend who's got a girl friend who's into astrology, the kind of person who asks you what your sign is before they say hello. That's it, 'a good friend of mine studies the stars.' In fact, in the first verse, it's 'a good friend of mine *follows* the stars,' so it could be ambiguous, a groupie or an astrologer.

"I didn't even know they were our neighbouring planets. I just thought of naming any two planets. What were the first that came to mind? I

(INSET) PAUL AND LINDA IN HAMBURG BISTRO.

ROCO
Hero
ROCO
Hero

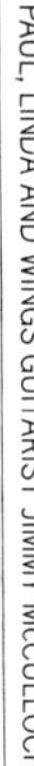
PAUL, LINDA AND WINGS GUITARIST JIMMY McCULLOCH.

thought, Jupiter, no, that doesn't fit . . . Saturn . . . no . . . Venus and Mars . . . that's great, I'll just put those in. Later, it turns out they've just done an eclipse, Venus and Mars have lined themselves up for the first time in something like a thousand years. I didn't know they were the gods of love and war, either, and I wasn't thinking about the Botticelli picture someone (George Melly) asked about."

McCartney also denied that the venues mentioned in 'Rock Show,' the second song on the first side of the album, constituted a cryptic reference to his tour plans with Wings.

"That just happens to coincide. I start off with an idea. 'Rock Show,' boom. Concert Gebauw came into my mind, because that's one of the places you play in Amsterdam. We played there (during Wings' 1973 European tour), so I rhymed it with 'Rock Show' in an English pronounciation of Gebauw. 'Long hair' . . . well, where else? Madison Square. 'Rock and roll' . . . well, that rhymes with Hollywood Bowl. Often these things that turn out to be great afterwards are just searches for a rhyme. I could see how you might think, well, he's doing this . . . but for me it's just writing a song. But as it happens, yes, I'd like to play those places, sure."

He said this with the confidence of a man sure of his band. "We'd like to have the band out in Britain this summer, have a bit of time off to write some more, and then really get it together for autumn. I keep saying we're coming to America, but we're planning and really want to.

"It's funny. Henry McCullough left and we got in Jimmy McCulloch. We lose a drummer named Geoff Britton, who's English, and get in a drummer called Joe English, who's American."

The new musicians had to be prepared to play in styles other than conventional rock-and-roll. 'You Gave Me the Answer' sounded born and bred in the big band era, when Paul McCartney wore tie and tails and his debutante sweetheart Linda wore floor-length gowns.

"I know it's sort of a rock-and-roll album but there's other things I like that aren't necessarily rock-and-roll," the artist explained. "On this LP I thought I'd like to get some of that in, so 'You Gave Me the Answer' is real fruity, imagining tie and tails, my impression of the Fred Astaire era.

"When I started to listen to music, the kind of music was Fred Astaire and the Billy Cotton Band Show (BBC radio), Cole Porter's type of lyrics. I like the Astaire films they show now on television. I think, wow, great, boy, can they dance! Boy, can they arrange tunes. They were only doing what we're doing now, but some of the time they were much better at it! Think of the choreographing of some of the big numbers, you just won't see that these days. We all know it's the money they had, but the class is still there for someone like myself to look back on and say 'That's a great idea.'

"I remember I was up in Liverpool once, just mucking around with this type of thing. If you play guitar, you like to do impressions. And I was singing an old tune and my Auntie Millie said to

WITH ARTHUR ASKEY AT AWARDS PRESENTATION LUNCH.

me, 'You know, that's just like Jack Buchanan!' He was one of my favourites, old Jack, I used to like all those blokes." (The British Buchanan was a star of stage musicals who also appeared in an Astaire film).

"I thought, great, she doesn't think it's a con, it's just a different style of singing, and she likes it. And I must admit, I do, it's very romantic. A fruity approach, but I'm not against all that."

Part of McCartney's genius has long been his ability to make a fascinating story out of a mundane experience. Watching a movie on television inspired that Astaire-like 'You Gave Me the Answer.' 'Penny Lane' may only have been a boring Liverpool street, but McCartney and Lennon made it sound like the home of intriguing individuals. The simple act of going to the corner market gave him the idea for 'Magneto and Titanium Man.'

"Yes, that's about Marvel Comics. When we were on holiday in Jamaica, we'd go into the supermarket every Saturday, when they got a new stock of comics in. I didn't use to read comics from eleven onwards, I thought I'd grown out of them, but I came back to them a couple of years ago. The drawings are great. I think you'll find that in twenty years time some of the guys drawing them were little Picassos. I think it's very clever how they do it. I love the names, I love the whole comic book thing."

"And I've been reading a bit of science fiction, things like *Foundation* by Asimov. I love the scope of it, the vision of it, because you can write anything. The second time 'Venus and Mars' comes around, it says 'Sitting in the hall of the Great Cathedral/Waiting for the transport to

WITH DENNY LAINE AND AWARDS FOR 'RED ROSE SPEEDWAY' AND 'BAND ON THE RUN'.

REHEARSAL IN STOCKHOLM, 1972.

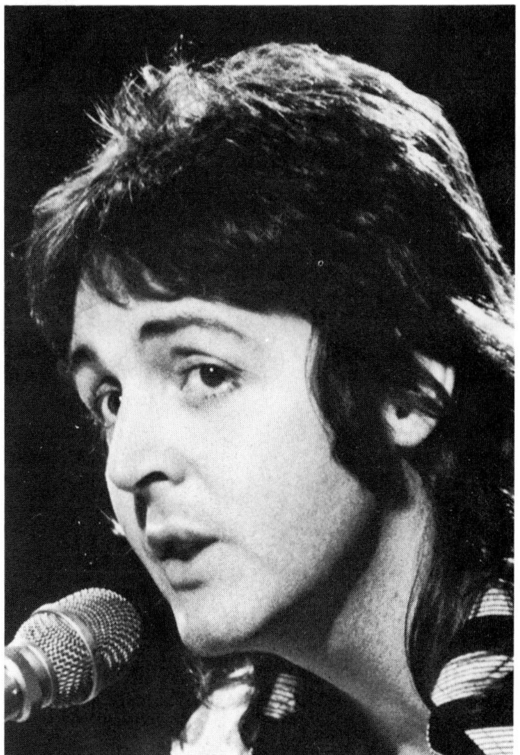

'TOP OF THE POPS' TV SHOW.

come.' That's like in science fiction books, waiting for the space shuttle. 'Starship 21ZNA9,' that's the kind of thing you'll find in Asimov. I like that, sitting in the Cathedral, really waiting for the saucer to come down, to take him off to Venus and Mars or whatever."

Magneto, Titanium Man and the Crimson Dynamo were all villains from the Marvel Comics post office wall. Joining them in the minds of most British rock fans are the little men of the Musicians Union and civil service who limit BBC Radio One's output of rock recordings to thirty-five hours a week. The needletime has been concentrated in the daytime, with the subsequent emphasis on a host of children's and housewives' favourites who never made it in the States, while artists like Jethro Tull and Led Zeppelin are hardly heard in any form. Even though he personally enjoys frequent airplay, McCartney shared his fellow rockers' angst.

"We don't have much good radio here in England, as you know. I was talking about this with one of the top men at EMI and I said that the BBC should have a station that plays the good stuff, Stones tracks, Beatles tracks, Zeppelin, what people want to hear. They say they don't have the needletime to play the good stuff, but that's not a good reason, they could just use the needletime differently.

"If you don't want kids to go underground, you've got to give them something they can like. BBC have never had enough of the good stuff. When I was a kid there was only one hour a week, and that coincided with one of my dad's favourite shows, and we had to fight it out in a friendly way every week to figure out who got to

listen. You could figure that today they could give up some of their Gardening Tips time for Led Zeppelin. But the man from EMI just smiled and said 'Oh, you'll never get *that* in England, old chap.' What an attitude, 'you'll never get *that* in England.' The attitude is the only reason it's never been done!"

McCartney does have a personal reason for feeling less than content with the British establishment, and that is the tax burden he is forced to carry as a top-grossing pop star. For tax purposes "we had to record outside the country. I have to write all my songs outside the country, too. Otherwise the government will say, right, this is a British record, all the money has to come back into Britain. I'm in 98m per cent tax then. I get 2p, the government gets 98p. I mean, I don't particularly like it when the (US) government gets 30¢ and I get 70¢ but it's better than getting 2p in the pound."

Yet for all this travail the Liverpudlian remains, in his own words, "British to the core," so much so that he even calls his American wife "honorary British." "I wouldn't leave. So many people are leaving and trying to make it look like they're not leaving. Rod's leaving for a year, I think that's bad management advice. Elton would never leave for good, he's totally English."

McCartney's Anglophelia is so great that he felt compelled to speak out against British membership in the Common Market shortly before the June, 1975 referendum. His comments to one national newspaper were printed in a column so personally derisive to Paul that his publicist was briefly suspended in recognition of the public relations disaster. With members of the music press he was also open in his dislike for the European Economic Community.

"One of the worst things about the Common Market is that miles are going to become kilometers," he protested. "That's a foreign word, another foreign word in the British language. Acres became hectares, and so on. I wouldn't mind if the British government announced we're gonna have these words, but they're still going to be English things. That pees me right off. You have a great tradition in England, and some people hate tradition. They seem to want to take it down and put something in its place. I think that people who do that without regard to the past and the validity of the tradition often make mistakes and come back in two years and think 'Blimey I wrecked that!' Whoever's going to

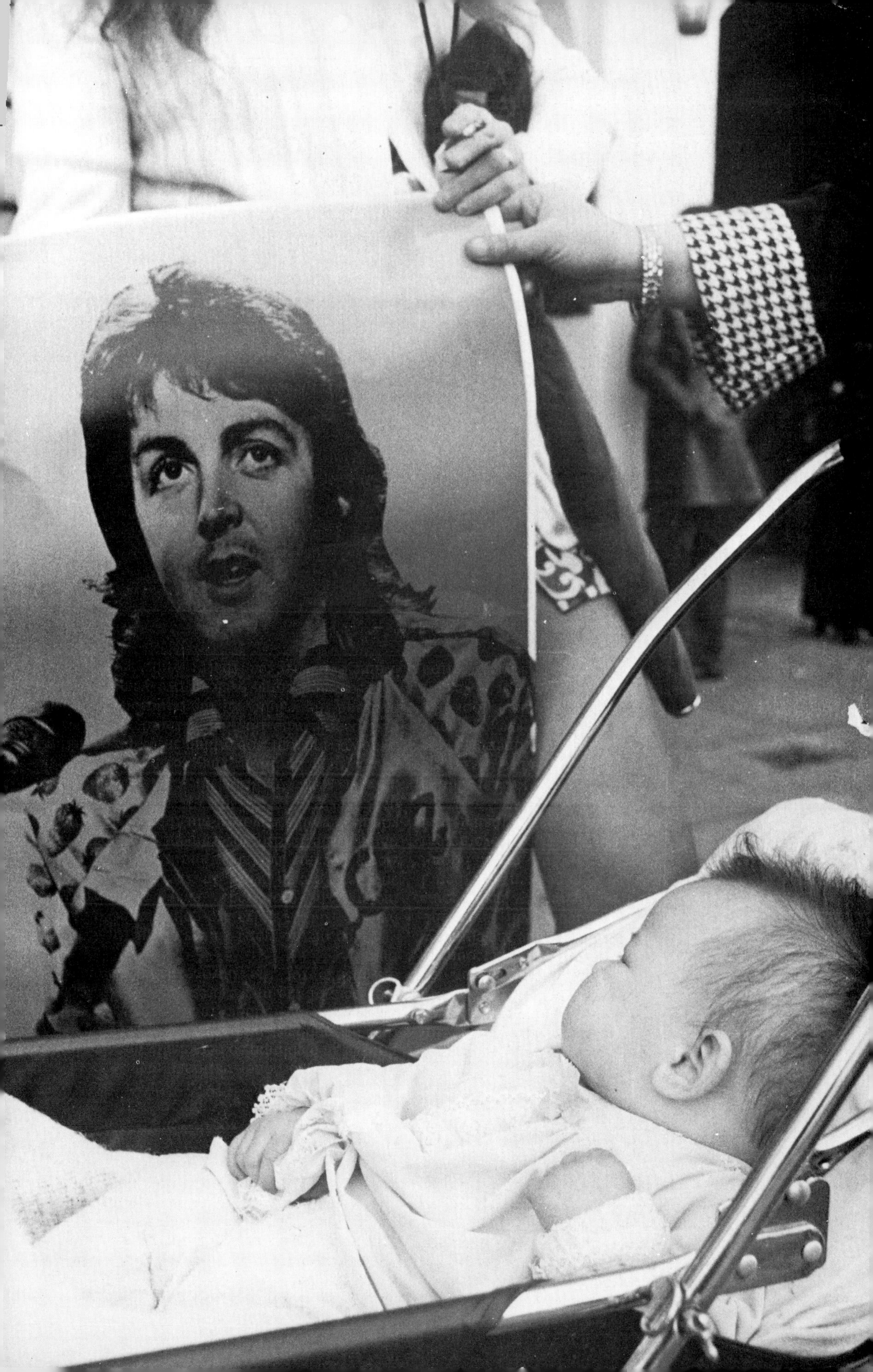

change kilometers from miles is going to be reading a book in ten years and say 'Ah, miles, they were good, weren't they?'

"I was reading a book about Egypt recently, some of it has gone into the new album ('Spirits of Ancient Egypt'). Apparently a measurement almost exactly the same as the inch was used in the construction of the pyramids. I'd hazard a guess that the millimeter isn't even that clever a measurement. I understand that it's more modern and it's easier, being in tens, but it's not for me. We had enough invaders and we finally got the British language straight, except for the normal amount of slang. I don't think we need to immediately go over to kilometers, hectares, kilos, liters, and to tell you the truth, I haven't even bothered to go to the trouble to learn all that stuff, it annoys me so much."

Despite the intensity of his views, McCartney did refrain from participating in the organized campaigning each side did in the weeks before the referendum. A movement to draft popular musicians into the fray failed, although Tim Rice, author of *Jesus Christ, Superstar,* did go on the BBC in support of British membership.

Paul manifested his strong British roots yet again on the closing track of 'Venus and Mars'. He recorded Tony Hatch's 'Crossroads,' theme of a long-running Independent Television Network drama-cum-soap opera series. "It is a bit of a British joke that I thought might be too much of a British joke, but I'd still like to put it out. If you don't get the joke on it, it sounds like a closing theme. Sort of like 'Ladies and Gentlemen, Miss Diana Ross!' and Diana walks off with the orchestra going (sings a triumphant exit song). . . But if you see the joke, it comes after 'Lonely Old People,' nobody asked us to play, they're wondering what's going on, spending time, nobody gets involved with lonely old people. One of the big things for lonely old people in England is to watch *Crossroads*. That was it, just a joke at the end. Funnily enough, they're going to use it at the end of the program now, use our tune on it, which is great."

ITV did indeed adopt the Wings version of 'Crossroads' as the closing theme of the program in the summer of 1975. Early in the summer the group appeared on television themselves in one-minute filmed commercials for the new album, shooting billiards in a Holland Park home. Two Wings television programs were being edited for broadcast in the 1975-76 season.

"The first is from when we had Geoff Britton

SCENE FROM 'JAMES PAUL McCARTNEY' TV SHOW.

GEORGE HARRISON WITH PAUL, LINDA AND HEATHER.

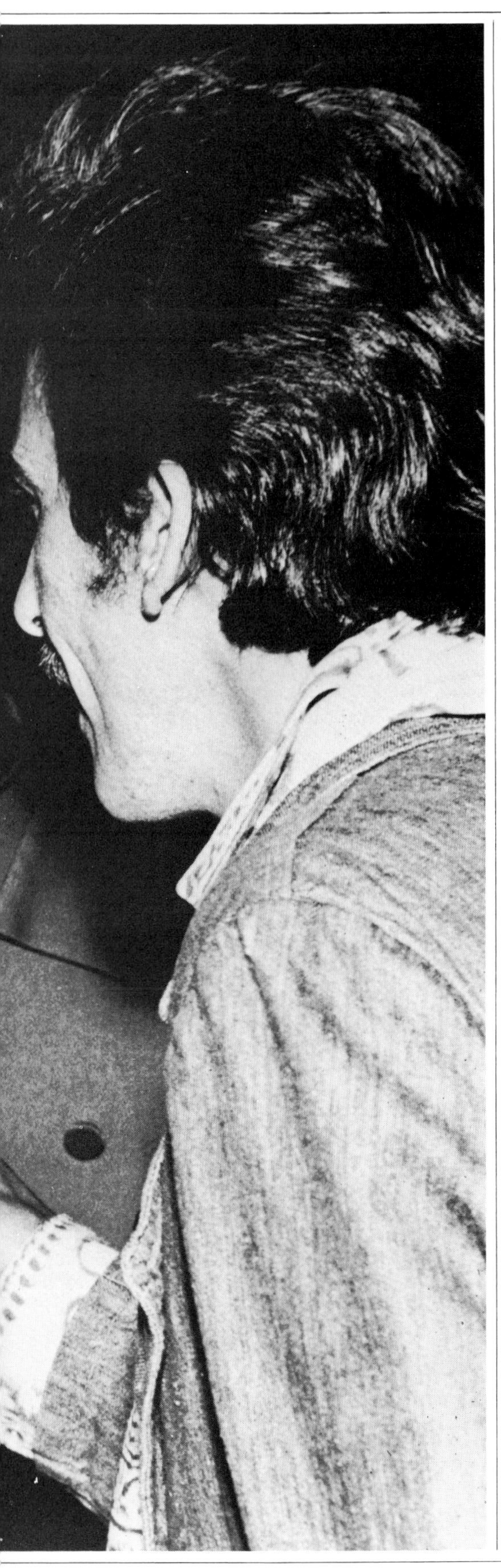

as drummer. We were rehearsing in Nashville and we just went into a studio and filmed the numbers we had been rehearsing. That's being put together now with the name 'One Hand Clapping. It's just us playing with a couple of things of chat, it's very simple.

"The other thing we've had for a couple of years now and are just finishing. It's sort of a children's thing, although we showed it to Steve Stills and he thought it was 8:00 prime time material. But I have a feeling that if it goes out 8:00 prime time people are going to say 'Oh, they could have done something better, it's an old line-up of Wings.' It's quite a nice thing, though, it's certainly better than, say, the news."

The increased interest in television as a promotional medium was just part of McCartney's decided emphasis on dealing with professionals. Well into his thirties, the rocker was now clearly working with show business giants and business experts. His manager was British entertainment world veteran Brian Brolly, his American lawyer New Yorker Lee Eastman, Linda's father. George Melly was commissioned to write the feature article in the 'Venus and Mars' press kit, while Peggy Lee was the recent beneficiary of a McCartney original, 'Let's Love.' He also delegated important decisions concerning the merchandising of his songs to Capitol Record's Al Coury. McCartney modestly gave the credit for *Band on the Run's* three-time appearance in the number one spot on the American chart to Coury's advice.

"I must not take the credit on *Band on the Run.* Al Coury, Capitol's ace plugger, rang up and told us 'I persuaded Pink Floyd to take 'Money' off *Dark Side of the Moon* as a single, and you want to know how many units we sold? We want 'Band on the Run'! We want 'Jet'! We want 'em off!' And he's such a good spieler, this fella, that I'll say, well, it sounds like sense. No skin off my nose, try it, and it just kept coming back up, much to my delight.

"With the Beatles we had a whole line of singles and it was very much a singley thing. When we had *Band on the Run*, we had a purist thing and said no, we're not going to trail it with a single, everybody does that, everybody pulls bloody singles off albums. We won't do that. We'll just release an LP.

"We released it and it didn't get much notice. A few people heard it and said, oh, that's quite nice, it went up to number seven and then started to plummet. I said oh, blimey, it's better than that! It could just be the physical fact that people haven't heard it.

"You suddenly realize that *everyone* is housewives, clerks, just people. The majority of people are not people from the record business, like we'd think, because that's the kind of people we meet. The majority of people don't know *Band on the Run* is out unless there's a single. If someone says 'This is the single from *Band on the Run*, then everyone knows it's out. That's the power of the single. You go into a shop and they say 'Well, it's on an album, do you want that,' and they say 'Oh, is it?' The communicative value of a single is the big thing.

"That's why we turned 'Junior's Farm' over to 'Sally G.' Some people think, blimey, they're just trying to get two records out of one. But I think that if it's a song that people would like to know and sing, and it gets played only by the people who buy the record, then I like to see if we can give it an extra plug.

"So that's what we were thinking. We weren't thinking it would be a hit again, we just wanted to expose the song. You get things like, twenty years later someone says 'That's the brilliant B-side of Joni Mitchell,' but people don't know it! If it had been exposed, it might have been a great big hit or a thing that lived in everyone's minds."

'Sally G' was promoted as a country single as well as a pop record by Capitol, as was 'Country Dreamer.' the B-side of 'Helen Wheels,' "When I'm in a place, it's not uncommon for me to want to write about where I am," Paul mused, now well-mellowed in London's late afternoon. "Elton John did 'Philadelphia Freedom,' you know. You see a lot of that, someone will turn up and write a song the next day. Being in Nashville, I wanted to use a couple of local guys. I never worked with a Nashville steel guitar player, and I had to have a bit of material I could bring in and ask them to do. This bloke named Buddy took us out to Printer's Alley, which is a little club district. There were a few people just playing country music, and we imagined a bit more than we had seen for 'Sally G'.

"A lot of people do that. I saw the documentary on David Hockney last night (BBC's *David Hockney in Paris*) in which he saw a Macy's ad, which to him seemed a perfect room. So he took the room and just painted a nude boy on it. He made one of his pictures out of it.

"I didn't see anyone named 'Sally G' when I was in Printer's Alley, nor did I see anyone who ran her eyes over me when she was singing 'A Tangled Mind.' That was my imagination, adding something to it, the reality of it." It was while in Nashville that McCartney first heard Jimmy McCulloch play 'Medicine Jar,' which he liked so much he included in the album.

'Sally G' was listed in the trade charts as the flip side of 'Junior's Farm' when the latter number was in the top ten, a rare distinction for a B-side that Wings had also achieved with 'Hi Hi Hi/C Moon' in Britain. There the occasion was a bit more infamous, since the BBC banned 'Hi Hi Hi,' and only played 'C Moon' while other stations played 'Hi Hi Hi,' resulting in the double chart placing.

'Junior's Farm/C Moon' was Wings' seventh consecutive top ten hit, a string extended to eight with 'Listen to What the Man Said.' It was America's longest top ten streak, with Elton John the nearest competitor with seven. McCartney's commercial appeal has not been equalled on this yardstick in the seventies.

It is hardest to believe that Wings have done thus by remaining virtually exclusively a studio act. Paul McCartney has not appeared on an American concert stage since the Beatles closed their 1966 tour in San Francisco. Wings 'Take One' played UK college dates in 1972, starting with the famous unannounced Nottingham performance, and then did selected British cities in 1973 to tie in with the release of 'Red Rose Speedway'. Yet these were low key appearances, devoid of sensational effects, major supporting act, and much of a sense of occasion. The largest capacity hall on the tour seated 4,000, hardly a test of an ex-Beatle's drawing power.

What was happening was that McCartney, fully aware that he would be reviewed in exactly that ex-Beatle light, was getting his feet wet as a Wing. The group deliberately performed no Lennon-McCartney numbers, and the Wings tours were thus literally the concert unveiling of a new band. We wrote this in the June 21, 1973 edition of ROLLING STONE:

Paul McCartney and Wings
New Theatre
May 12th, 1973

"Look, there goes someone with black hair! Is that a Wing?" asked one of the four twelve-year olds camped at the New Theatre six hours before show time.

"No, outside of Paul McCartney none of them has dark black hair," answered her friend with the David Cassidy button and McCartney picture. She then turned to the inquisitive reporter. "Listen, we're a little young to remember the Beatles. We've heard of them, but we're here because we're Wings fans."

"My favourite Paul McCartney songs?" a third girl reflected. "I'd say 'C Moon,' 'Hi Hi Hi,' and 'My Love.' "

There were no Lennon-McCartney songs and no mention of the Beatles when Paul McCartney and Wings played the second concert of their first full-fledged British tour. Those who expected to hear ballads, Beatles or bubblegum were confounded. The group came on stage in black outfits and played a set of rock numbers interrupted only by the recent soft-sounding hits 'C Moon,' 'My Love,' and 'Live and Let Die.'

Although McCartney played spokesman between the first few numbers, the Wings concert was not just his show. When Henry McCullough announced it was time for "a real blast from the past," Denny Laine proceeded to sing 'Go Now,' his 1965 hit with the Moody Blues. Laine remained featured vocalist on his composition, 'Say You Don't Mind,' a 1971 British top ten success for Colin Blunstone.

The concert became a battle of nerves as McCartney politely suggested before each number that the audience make some noise. It held out until he remarked that since two "real rockers" were finishing the show it might be time for everyone to "shake your bums or whatever."

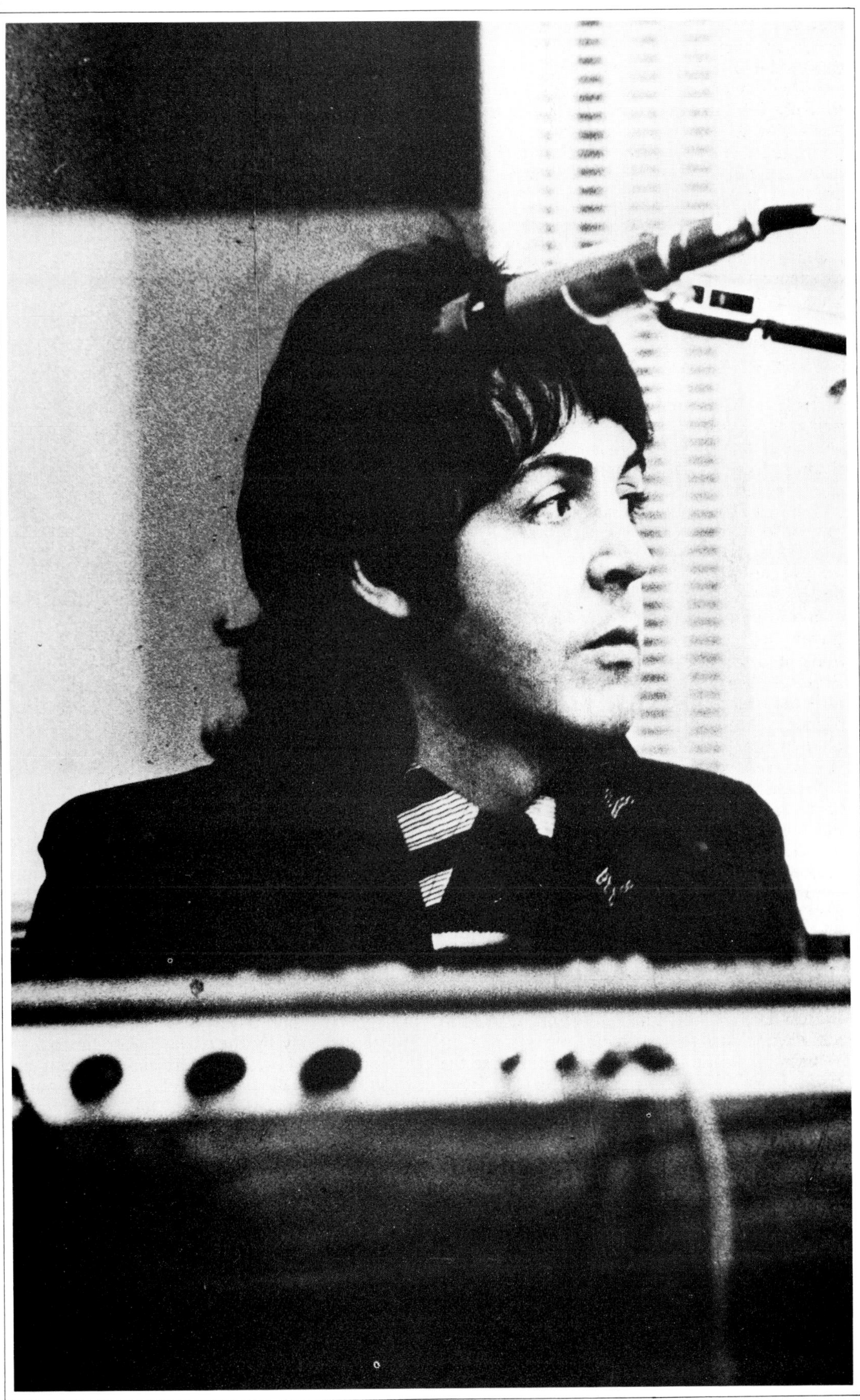

On the first chord five persons stood up and that broke the Oxford reserve. Within 20 seconds almost everyone was on their feet, half the crowd was rushing forward and two zealots leaped onstage. The closer, 'Hi Hi Hi,' and the surprise encore, 'Long Tall Sally,' were exercises in near-pandemonium.

Wings won over its audience with compact rock tunes. There were few visual effects, no long monologues and no extended solos. Linda McCartney, whom some observers have considered to be Wings' extra added detraction, almost acquitted herself. It was only when Paul replaced her on keyboards and she was reduced to shaking a tambourine and looking uncomfortable that she seem extraneous.

It was a respectable concert. Wings don't rate raves yet, but the time for snickering is over.

Only by accumulating a post-Beatle repertoire has McCartney been able to face the prospects of performing Beatle songs live again. Unlike his 1973 dates, Wings concerts in late 1975 and 1976 include passing reference to the body of what has gone before.

"We've been getting numbers together in Rye, rehearsing in the South of England. We're OK now, because we've got *Band on the Run, Venus and Mars,* and all the singles," Paul said in late May. "We have to think about what people want to hear me sing. I suppose they might want to hear me sing 'Hey Jude,' so I should do it. We're trying to think of which of those old numbers we could do. I'm thinking people might want to hear 'The Long and Winding Road,' 'Hey Jude,' 'Let It Be,' 'Fool on the Hill,' maybe, 'Blackbird,' and 'Yesterday.' I

HARRY NILSSON, RINGO, PAUL AND LINDA.

STILL FROM TV COMMERCIAL FOR 'VENUS AND MARS'.

don't think I could get away with not doing 'Yesterday.'

"But I don't like to commit us to doing anything too specific too soon. We like to say we want to do something, but we don't want to have to do it in case something goes wrong at the last minute. We like to reserve that freedom for ourselves."

The last flurry of Beatle reunion rumours died in early 1974, after the release of the 'Ringo' album featuring compositions from Harrison, Lennon and McCartney had failed to generate a get-together either in studio or on stage. The Beatle period receives only slight mention in the new McCartney biography prepared by McCartney Productions for any sort of Who's Who which now requests his listing. This official new version emphasizes the Wings phase of his career:

McCartney, James Paul, M.B.E.
British, born 18th June, 1942.
Musician, Artist, Composer.
Former member of the Beatles
(disbanded, 1970).
Formed own group Wings 1971 and toured
Europe and UK 1972/73
Composer:
Soundtrack music for the feature film 'The
Family Way' (1966).
theme song for 'Live and Let Die'
(1973) nominated for Academy Award.
Films:
'A Hard Day's Night (1964),
'Help' (1965),
'Let It Be' (1970).
Television:
'Magical Mystery Tour' (1967),
'James Paul McCartney' (1973).
Albums:
'McCartney' (1970),
'Ram' (1971),
'Wings Wild Life' (1971),
'Red Rose Speedway' (1973),
'Band on the Run' (1973),
'Venus and Mars' (1975),
(1975 received two US Grammy Awards
for 'Band on the Run' including Best Pop
Vocal Performance).
Wife:
Linda Eastman (American).
Three daughters:
Heather, Mary and Stella.
Business:
McCartney Productions Limited, London W.1.

The three daughters mentioned at the end of the official biographical listing are far more familiar with their father's career as a Wing than as a Beatle. Stella shocked us across the generation gap when she pointed to our blue Beatles' 10th Anniversary t-shirt at Elton John's June, 1975 Wembley concert. "That's Ringo!" she exclaimed, pointing both to the likeness of Mr. Starkey and the man joking with her father a few feet away. "And that's Daddy! But who's that?"

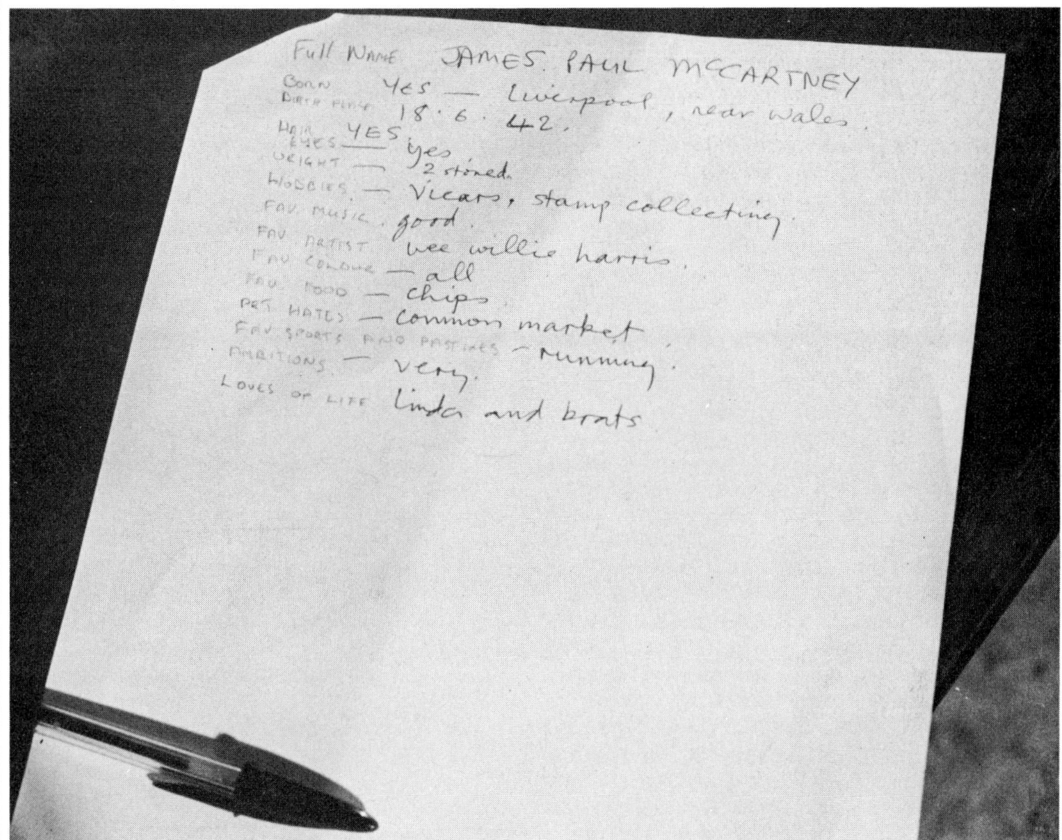
Full Name JAMES PAUL McCARTNEY
Born YES — Liverpool, near Wales.
Birth place 18 · 6 · 42.
Hair YES
Eyes — yes
Weight — 2 stoned.
Hobbies — Vicars, stamp collecting.
Fav. music good.
Fav artist wee willie harris.
Fav colour — all
Fav food — chips.
Pet hates — common market
Fav sports and pastimes — running.
Ambitions — very.
Loves of life Linda and brats.

She was pointing to the picture of John Lennon.

The children go with their parents on their recording jaunts which, as McCartney explained, had to be out of Britain for tax reasons. "I don't think it's bad on the kids," he stated. "What we do is, whenever we get someplace, we immediately try to set it up as homey as possible. Plus, there are always good people around. And a pool in L.A., Mardi Gras in New Orleans – these are good places for children. It's great for the kids."

The unshakingly strong family life McCartney enjoys is so unusual for the pop world it is an angle for the conventional media to focus on. *People* did so in its early 1975 cover story. McCartney acknowledged it as a far cry from his swinging batchelor life during the early Beatle days, and the hearth constitutes yet another break from the past.

So did the death of Pete Ham, the Badfinger songwriter who took his own life by hanging in his lonely Golders Green room in the spring of 1975. McCartney had written the group's first hit, 'Come and Get It' from *The Magic Christian*, after which Ham and his comrades took over for the international hits 'No Matter What,' 'Day After Day,' and 'Baby Blue.' Ham co-wrote 'Without You,' Nilsson's number one single, which originally appeared on an Apple Badfinger album.

"Did you hear about Pete Ham?" McCartney said. "I was sad because he was good. Well, I told everybody he was good. It was one of those things where you hear about it and think, if only I had called him up a week earlier, I wonder if I could have helped to save him?"

Linda nodded in understanding. "It was like that with Jimi (Hendrix). The week before he died we were talking about him and decided we had to invite him up to Scotland, but we didn't that night. A week later, he was dead."

Ham's death further scattered to the winds the Apple artists of the hopeful late sixties. Only James Taylor, now on Warner Brothers, and Billy Preston, currently recording for A&M, are still enjoying commercial success. McCartney himself cut his link with the label in 1975 by adopting the Capitol logo of the fifties for his releases. The first Wings records to bear the new old label were *Venus and Mars* and 'Listen to What the Man Said.'

Indeed, instead of listing ways in which McCartney has moved away from his first historic role, one more appropriately tries to find factors which have not changed. They are hard to identify. His songwriting partner has lived in a different country for years. He has changed managers several times while maintaining the American connection with his wife's father. There are different labels on his records. He makes his records outside the country he used to make them in, using different session men to complement Wings and producing himself rather than relying on George Martin. Unlike other phoenix bird rockers of the seventies, Paul McCartney has come back not from drugs or obscurity but from his historic self.

11/96 (26421)

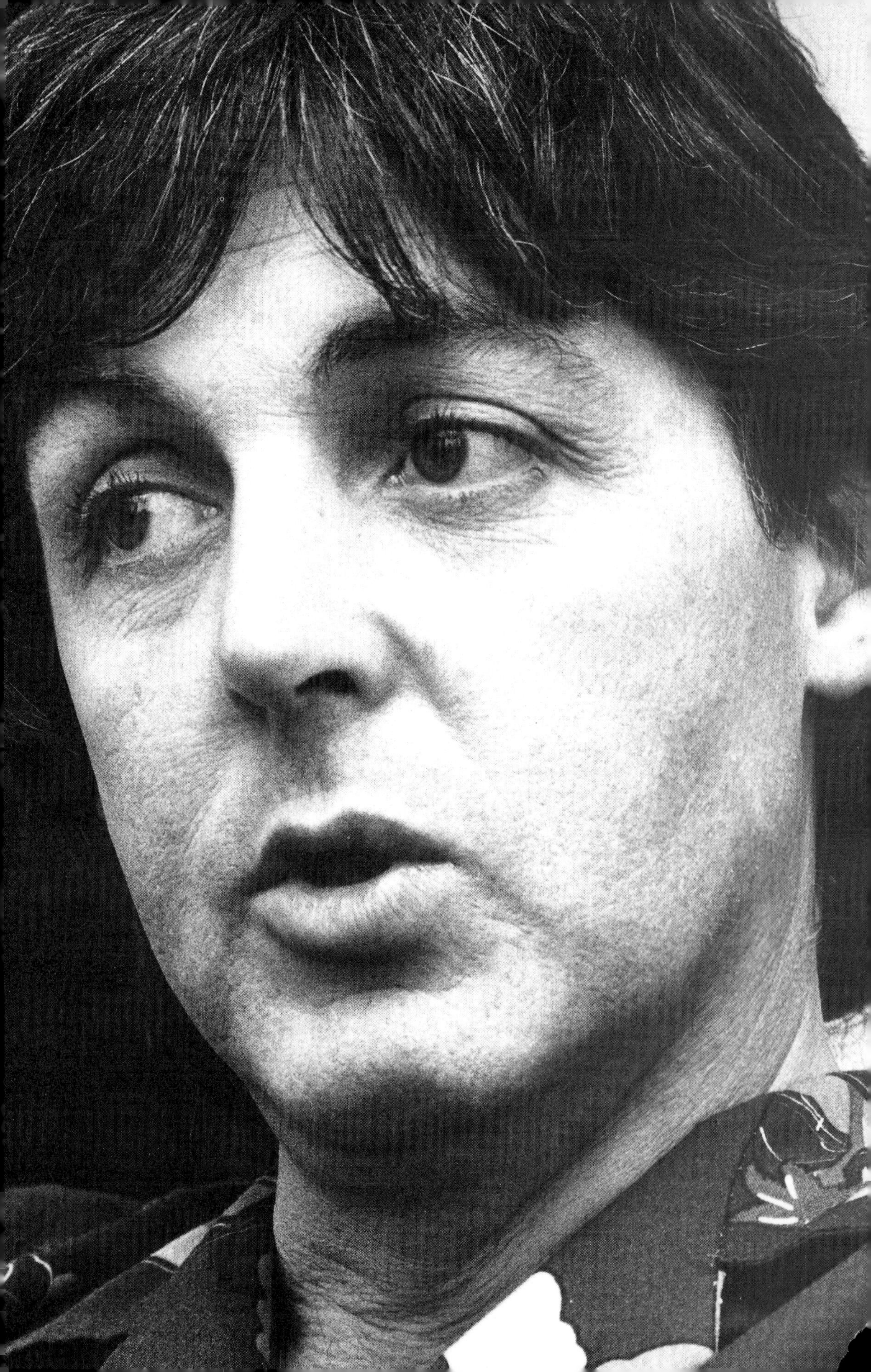